GW01458243

Teaching writing skills

Read — Analyse — Plan

Primary writing

Narratives

Recounts

Reports

Procedures

Explanations

Discussions

6264C

PRIMARY WRITING *(Book E)*

Published by Prim-Ed Publishing 2008
Reprinted under licence by Prim-Ed Publishing 2008
Copyright© R.I.C. Publications® 2006
ISBN 978-1-84654-109-4
PR–6264

Additional titles available in this series:
PRIMARY WRITING *(Book A)*
PRIMARY WRITING *(Book B)*
PRIMARY WRITING *(Book C)*
PRIMARY WRITING *(Book D)*
PRIMARY WRITING *(Book F)*
PRIMARY WRITING *(Book G)*

Internet websites
In some cases, websites or specific URLs may be recommended. While these are checked and rechecked at the time of publication, the publisher has no control over any subsequent changes which may be made to webpages. It is *strongly* recommended that the class teacher checks *all* URLs before allowing pupils to access them.

View all pages online

Website: www.prim-ed.com

Primary writing

Foreword

Primary writing is a series of seven books designed to provide opportunities for pupils to read, examine and write a variety of text types; narratives, recounts, procedures, reports, explanations and discussions.

Titles in this series:

- *Primary writing* Book A
- *Primary writing* Book B
- *Primary writing* Book C
- *Primary writing* Book D
- *Primary writing* Book E
- *Primary writing* Book F
- *Primary writing* Book G

This book is also provided in digital format on the accompanying CD.

Contents

Teachers notes

Six text types have been chosen:
- narratives
- recounts
- procedures
- reports
- explanations
- discussions

Three examples of each text type are given for pupils to read and analyse.

Following each example, a framework is provided for pupils to use in planning and writing that text type.

Each text type is presented over four pages:

~ teachers page

~ pupil page – 1 includes an example of the text type

~ pupil page – 2 uses a framework for analysing the text type on pupil page – 1

~ pupil page – 3 provides a framework for the pupil to write his or her own example of the particular text type

Teachers page

The text type and number of the example are given.

The parts of each text type are given with relevant information for the teacher.

Teacher information provides suggestions for using the worksheet in the classroom and ideas for display, publishing, purposes for writing, appropriate audiences and the context in which pupils may be asked to write the particular text type.

Some examples of language features used in each text type are indicated. Also see pages vi – vii.

Answers are provided for pupil page – 2 where the pupils are analysing the text type.

Pupil pages

Pupil page – 1

The text type and number of the example are given.

The text type example is supplied.

Artwork appropriate to the example is provided.

Narrative 1

Cup final hero!

Richard Riggs and Brian Bowen arrived early at Paul Peckham's house. This was the day the trio had dreamt of all season. Their football team, Robe Rockets, were in the final of the Northern Districts Cup, to be held at the local park. The boys had attended every training session, played in every match and, among them, had scored most of the goals. But even Richard and Brian had to agree, Paul Peckham was the star player.

Paul packed his lucky boots in his bag. He had worn them for every match this season and had scored 47 goals. He was hoping to reach the magic 50 with a half-trick today. With Paul's dog Romelyn at their heels, the boys set off for the park.

As they passed the end of the main street, a shout and a loud whizzing noise made them turn quickly. Before he realised what was happening, Paul was knocked to the ground and, as he fell, his bag was dragged from his arm. In a second, the assailant was gone.

'After him! Quickly! He's got my boots!' Paul cried in despair as he staggered up.

The boys ran after him but were no match for a thief on a skateboard. Romelyn, however, was up for the chase.

Tearing down pathways, jumping over walls and squeezing through fences, the fit dog was enjoying a great workout. The boy on the board had not expected a pursuer with such dogged determination. He climbed a tree in an effort to escape but Romelyn was on his scent and found him immediately.

The three boys followed the sound of familiar barking and waited at the base of the tree, while the boy sheepishly climbed down.

'Sorry', he mumbled. 'I was just having a laugh.'

'Well, we need someone to look after Romelyn while we play our match and I think he's decided that someone is you', declared Paul. 'Come on, or we'll be late!'

In the closing minutes of what had been a nail-biting match, the score was level at two all. Paul's lucky boots had kicked two goals. A foul from the opposing team gave Robe Rockets a penalty and a chance for the Cup, and for Paul Peckham, the chance of reaching the magic 50. The spectators hushed as he prepared to take his kick. Just as his foot made contact with the ball, Romelyn barked wildly. Time stood still. Would the ball find the back of the net?

The referee blew the whistle for the end of the match, the tournament and the season. The crowd went berserk. Paul Peckham was carried at shoulder height by his team.

'Robe Rockets are the champions', screamed the voice through the loud hailer. 'Three cheers for the champions and the lucky boots of Paul Peckham! Hip hip ...'

Questions are given to help pupils to **identify particular parts of a text type framework**. The questions may also be used to assess pupil knowledge of a particular framework.

Pupil page – 2

Examining narrative 1

Use the narrative on page 3 to complete the page.

1. Title
Give reasons for both Paul Peckham and Romelyn being a 'Cup final hero'.

Paul Peckham	Romelyn

2. Orientation
(a) What are you told about the main characters?

(b) When and where does the Cup final match take place?

3. Complication and events
Briefly describe the problem and how it happened.

4. Resolution
(a) Who solved the problem and how?

(b) How did the assailant pay for his deed?

5. Conclusion
(a) What are the three main points of the conclusion?

(b) Write an addition to the conclusion about the boy on the skateboard.

Pupil page – 3

The text type and plan number are given.

A suggested text type **topic** has been chosen for pupils. (Blank frameworks for each text type can be found on pages xiv – xix.)

Narrative plan 1

1. Plan a narrative based on a sports story.

Title

Orientation

Complication and events

Resolution

Conclusion

2. Write your narrative.

3. Edit your work.

The framework for writing the text type is provided for pupils to follow.

Pupils are encouraged to **proofread** their work.

• **Pupil page – 1** may be used at a later date to identify specific spelling, grammar or punctuation examples, as a reading comprehension activity or reading assessment.

Writing format information

Below are general descriptions of the text types included in this book.

Report
– is a framework which describes aspects of a living or non-living thing in detail
– includes:
  • **Title**
  • **Classification**: a general or classifying statement
  • **Description**: accurate and detailed
  • **Conclusion**: a comment about the content of the report (optional)
– uses the following **language features**:
  • factual language rather than imaginative
  • the third person
  • the timeless present tense
  • information organised into paragraphs

A report may be written in the form of a book review, scientific report, newspaper or magazine article, eyewitness account or a progress report.

Recount
– is a framework which retells events as they happened in time order
– may be factual, personal or imaginative
– includes:
  • **Title**
  • **Orientation**: all relevant background (who, when, where, why)
  • **Events**: significant events in detail
  • **Conclusion**: often with an evaluative comment
– uses the following **language features**:
  • vocabulary to suggest time passing
  • paragraphs to show separate sections
  • the past tense

A recount may be written in the form of a newspaper report, diary, letter, journal, eyewitness account, biography, autobiography or history.

Narrative
– is a framework which tells a story
– includes:
  • **Title**
  • **Orientation**: the setting, time and characters
  • **Complication**: involving the main character(s) and a sequence of events
  • **Resolution**: to the complication
  • **Conclusion**: often showing what has changed and what the characters have learnt
– uses the following **language features**:
  • a range of conjunctions to connect ideas
  • appropriate paragraphing
  • descriptive language
  • usually written in past tense

A narrative may be written in the form of a poem, story, play, imaginative story, fairytale, novel, myth, legend, ballad, science fiction story or modern fantasy.

Procedure
– is a framework which outlines how something is made or done
– includes:
  • **Title**
  • **Goal**: the purpose of the procedure shown clearly and precisely
  • **Materials**: a list of materials or requirements under appropriate headings or layout
  • **Steps**: the method in a detailed, logical sequence
  • **Test**: an evaluation (if appropriate)
– uses the following **language features**:
  • instructions often with an imperative verb
  • subject-specific vocabulary
  • simple present tense
  • concise language

A procedure may be written in the form of a recipe, instructions for making something, an experiment, an instruction manual, a maths procedure, how to play a game, how to operate an appliance, how to use an atlas or how to deal with a problem.

Writing format information

Explanation

- is a framework which outlines how something occurs, works or is made
- includes:
  - **Title**
  - **Statement**: precisely what is to be explained
  - **Explanation**: a clear account in logical sequence of how and why the phenomenon occurs
  - **Conclusion**: an evaluation and comment about what has been explained

  OR

  - **Title**
  - a **definition**
  - a **description** of the components or parts
  - the operation—how it works or is made
  - the application—where and when it works or is applied
  - special features—interesting comments
  - evaluation or comment/**conclusion**
- uses the following **language features**:
  - subject-specific terms and technical vocabulary where appropriate
  - simple present tense is often used
  - linking words to show cause and effect
  - information is organised into paragraphs

An explanation may be written in the form of an essay, or a handbook—for example, how a kite works—a science, health or geography text.

Discussion

- is a framework which argues for a particular position and attempts to persuade the audience to share this view
- includes:
  - **Title**
  - **Overview**: statement of the problem or issue and the writer's position
  - **Arguments**: presented in a logical manner with supporting detail, usually from the strongest to the weakest
  - **Conclusion**: a restating of the writer's position and a summary of the arguments presented
- uses the following **language features**:
  - a variety of controlling and emotive words and conjunctions
  - paragraphs to state and elaborate on each point

A discussion may be written in the form of an essay, a letter, policy statement, a critical review, an advertisement, an editorial or a speech.

Modelled writing

The role of the teacher is to observe and support pupils as they develop as writers.

Writing is an extremely complex activity, simultaneously involving decisions on content, text coherence and cohesion, spelling, grammar, punctuation and a sense of audience and purpose. Because it takes time and practice to develop understanding of the writing process and the different writing formats, many opportunities for pupils to interact with their teacher and their peers are essential.

Modelled writing is an effective way of supporting pupil writers, particularly when the focus is on the cognitive processes involved.

Frequent modelling of the planning process and how these plans can be used to write text in different formats, is strongly recommended.

Writing format checklists

Pupil **narrative** checklist

☐ ☐ ☐ ☐ ☐ ☐ ☐ ☐ ☐ ☐ ☐ ☐ ☐ ☐

Title:

The title is appropriate and interesting.

Orientation:

The characters are introduced and described.

Information about where the story happened is provided.

The time the story took place is stated.

Complication and events:

The complication involving the main characters is explained.

The sequence of events is described.

Resolution:

A logical, believable resolution is presented.

Conclusion:

The narrative has a satisfactory ending.

Writing skills:

The narrative is written in the past tense.

Descriptive language is included.

Vocabulary is varied and interesting.

Different conjunctions connect ideas.

Paragraphs are used to introduce new ideas.

Punctuation and spelling have been checked.

Name: _____ Date: _____

Pupil **narrative** checklist

☐ ☐ ☐ ☐ ☐ ☐ ☐ ☐ ☐ ☐ ☐ ☐ ☐ ☐

Title:

The title is appropriate and interesting.

Orientation:

The characters are introduced and described.

Information about where the story happened is provided.

The time the story took place is stated.

Complication and events:

The complication involving the main characters is explained.

The sequence of events is described.

Resolution:

A logical, believable resolution is presented.

Conclusion:

The narrative has a satisfactory ending.

Writing skills:

The narrative is written in the past tense.

Descriptive language is included.

Vocabulary is varied and interesting.

Different conjunctions connect ideas.

Paragraphs are used to introduce new ideas.

Punctuation and spelling have been checked.

Name: _____ Date: _____

Writing format checklists

Pupil **recount** checklist

☐

Title:

☐ The title is suitable.

Orientation:

☐ A clearly written orientation provides relevant information about who, when, where and why.

Events:

☐ Significant events are described in detail.

☐ Events are retold in chronological order.

Conclusion:

☐ The ending is clearly described.

☐ An evaluative comment about the conclusion is included.

Writing skills:

☐ Paragraphs are used to show separate sections.

☐ Descriptive language is included.

☐ Vocabulary suggests the passing of time.

☐ The past tense is maintained.

☐ Sentence beginnings vary.

☐ Quotation marks are used for quoted speech.

☐ Punctuation and spelling have been checked.

Name: _____ Date: _____

Pupil **recount** checklist

☐

Title:

☐ The title is suitable.

Orientation:

☐ A clearly written orientation provides relevant information about who, when, where and why.

Events:

☐ Significant events are described in detail.

☐ Events are retold in chronological order.

Conclusion:

☐ The ending is clearly described.

☐ An evaluative comment about the conclusion is included.

Writing skills:

☐ Paragraphs are used to show separate sections.

☐ Descriptive language is included.

☐ Vocabulary suggests the passing of time.

☐ The past tense is maintained.

☐ Sentence beginnings vary.

☐ Quotation marks are used for quoted speech.

☐ Punctuation and spelling have been checked.

Name: _____ Date: _____

Writing format checklists

Pupil **report** checklist

☐ ☐ ☐ ☐   ☐   ☐ ☐ ☐ ☐ ☐ ☐ ☐ ☐

Title: _____

Classification:
A general or classifying statement about the subject of the report is included.

Description:
Accurate, detailed descriptions are provided.
Information is clearly presented.
Facts are relevant and interesting.

Conclusion:
A personal comment is made about the subject.

Writing skills:
Language is factual rather than imaginative.
The report is written in the third person.
Vocabulary suggests the passing of time.
The present tense is used.
Technical vocabulary and subject-specific terms are used.
Information is organised in paragraphs.
Punctuation and spelling have been checked.

Name: _____ Date: _____

Pupil **report** checklist

☐ ☐ ☐ ☐   ☐   ☐ ☐ ☐ ☐ ☐ ☐

Title: _____

Classification:
A general or classifying statement about the subject of the report is included.

Description:
Accurate, detailed descriptions are provided.
Information is clearly presented.
Facts are relevant and interesting.

Conclusion:
A personal comment is made about the subject.

Writing skills:
Language is factual rather than imaginative.
The report is written in the third person.
Vocabulary suggests the passing of time.
The present tense is used.
Technical vocabulary and subject-specific terms are used.
Information is organised in paragraphs.
Punctuation and spelling have been checked.

Name: _____ Date: _____

Writing format checklists

Pupil **procedure** checklist

Title: _____

Goal: ☐

The purpose is clearly and precisely stated.

Materials: ☐

The materials or requirements are listed under appropriate headings or layout.

Method: ☐ ☐ ☐

The steps are clear and concise.

There is a logical order to the sequence of the steps.

The steps are easy to understand and follow.

All the necessary steps are included.

Test: ☐

An evaluation to test if the procedure has been successfully followed is included.

Writing skills: ☐ ☐ ☐ ☐

Most instructions begin with command verbs.

The present tense is used.

Unnecessary words are omitted.

Punctuation and spelling have been checked.

Name: _____ Date: _____

Pupil **procedure** checklist

Title: _____

Goal: ☐

The purpose is clearly and precisely stated.

Materials: ☐

The materials or requirements are listed under appropriate headings or layout.

Method: ☐ ☐ ☐

The steps are clear and concise.

There is a logical order to the sequence of the steps.

The steps are easy to understand and follow.

All the necessary steps are included.

Test: ☐

An evaluation to test if the procedure has been successfully followed is included.

Writing skills: ☐ ☐ ☐ ☐

Most instructions begin with command verbs.

The present tense is used.

Unnecessary words are omitted.

Punctuation and spelling have been checked.

Name: _____ Date: _____

Writing format checklists

Pupil **explanation** checklist

Title: _____

Definition:
☐ A precise statement or definition is provided.

Description:
☐ A clear account of how and why the phenomenon occurs is included.
☐ Information is relevant and correct.
☐ Information is provided in a logical order.
☐ Explanations are clearly and simply stated.

Concluding statement:
☐ The conclusion includes an evaluation or comment.

Writing skills:
☐ Linking words are used to show cause and effect.
☐ The simple present tense is used.
☐ Technical vocabulary and subject-specific terms are used.
☐ Information is organised in paragraphs.
☐ Spelling and punctuation have been checked.

Name: _____ Date: _____

Pupil **explanation** checklist

Title: _____

Definition:
☐ A precise statement or definition is provided.

Description:
☐ A clear account of how and why the phenomenon occurs is included.
☐ Information is relevant and correct.
☐ Information is provided in a logical order.
☐ Explanations are clearly and simply stated.

Concluding statement:
☐ The conclusion includes an evaluation or comment.

Writing skills:
☐ Linking words are used to show cause and effect.
☐ The simple present tense is used.
☐ Technical vocabulary and subject-specific terms are used.
☐ Information is organised in paragraphs.
☐ Spelling and punctuation have been checked.

Name: _____ Date: _____

Writing format checklists

Pupil **discussion** checklist

□   □ □ □ □   □ □   □ □ □ □

Title: _____

Overview:
The opening statement presents the problem or issue and the writer's position.

Arguments:
Arguments are presented in a logical manner.
Supporting information is provided.
The strongest arguments are presented first.
The language is persuasive.

Conclusion:
A summary of the supporting arguments is given.
An evaluative comment is presented.

Writing skills:
Paragraphs state and elaborate each point.
Controlling and emotive language is used.
A variety of conjunctions is used.
Punctuation and spelling have been checked.

Name: _____   **Date:** _____

Pupil **discussion** checklist

□   □ □ □ □   □ □   □ □ □ □

Title: _____

Overview:
The opening statement presents the problem or issue and the writer's position.

Arguments:
Arguments are presented in a logical manner.
Supporting information is provided.
The strongest arguments are presented first.
The language is persuasive.

Conclusion:
A summary of the supporting arguments is given.
An evaluative comment is presented.

Writing skills:
Paragraphs state and elaborate each point.
Controlling and emotive language is used.
A variety of conjunctions is used.
Punctuation and spelling have been checked.

Name: _____   **Date:** _____

Blank writing format – Narrative

Title

Orientation

Who? When? Where? Why?

Complication and events

Resolution

How was it solved?

Conclusion

Blank writing format – Recount

Title

Orientation

Who? Where? When? Why?

Events

Conclusion

Blank writing format – Procedure

Title

Goal

Materials

Steps

Test

How will you know if your procedure works?

Blank writing format – Report

Title

Classification

What is it?

Description

Conclusion

What I think about it.

Blank writing format – Explanation

Title

Definition

What it is.

Description

Conclusion

What I think.

PRIMARY WRITING

Blank writing format – Discussion

Title

Overview

What is the topic?

What is my point of view?

Arguments

Conclusion

Proofreading and editing checklist

Name: _____ **Date:** _____

Title: _____ **Text type:** _____

Punctuation:

I have included:

- capital letters for:
    - beginning sentences. .... ☐
    - proper nouns. .... ☐
    - titles .... ☐
- question marks. .... ☐
- full stops. .... ☐
- commas. .... ☐
- apostrophes:
    - for grammatical contractions. .... ☐
    - to show ownership. .... ☐
- exclamation marks. .... ☐
- quotation marks. .... ☐

Spelling:

I have:

- checked the spelling of any unknown words. .... ☐
- not confused words that sound the same. .... ☐
- used correct ending for plurals. .... ☐

Language features:

I have included:

- a variety of different verbs. .... ☐
- correct verb tenses. .... ☐
- appropriate adverbs to describe verbs. .... ☐
- suitable nouns to name things, people, places and ideas. ... ☐
- appropriate pronouns .... ☐
- interesting adjectives in descriptions. .... ☐
- suitable conjunctions to connect ideas. .... ☐
- appropriate paragraphing. .... ☐

Writing:

I have read through my writing to check that:

- it makes sense. .... ☐
- it is easy to understand. .... ☐
- there are no repeated or omitted words. .... ☐
- there are no errors of fact. .... ☐

Class recording sheet

Date: ✓ developed • developing ✗ not yet	Pupils																																		
NARRATIVES																																			
Title is appropriate																																			
Characters are introduced																																			
Setting is described																																			
Complication is outlined																																			
Resolution is provided																																			
Conclusion is suitable																																			
RECOUNTS																																			
Reader is orientated																																			
Events are described																																			
Events are in correct order																																			
Conclusion is suitable																																			
PROCEDURES																																			
Goal is stated																																			
Materials are listed																																			
Steps are clear and sequenced																																			
Unnecessary words are omitted																																			
REPORTS																																			
Subject is classified																																			
Description is clear																																			
Facts are accurate																																			
A final comment is included																																			
EXPLANATIONS																																			
Subject is defined																																			
Explanation is clear																																			
Relevant information and vocabulary																																			
Order is logical																																			
DISCUSSIONS																																			
Topic and writer's position stated																																			
Arguments are logical and supported																																			
Language is persuasive																																			
Arguments and position summarised																																			
WRITING SKILLS																																			
Spells common words correctly																																			
Uses appropriate vocabulary																																			
Punctuation is usually correct																																			
Verb tense is correct																																			
Consistent ideas, sequenced correctly																																			
Shows sense of purpose and audience																																			
Edits and proofreads writing																																			

Curriculum links

England
Literacy – Writing (Texts)

Book	Year	Objectives
A	1	• plan writing and follow it through • use key features of narrative in their own writing • convey information and ideas in non-narrative forms • use new and interesting words and phrases, including story language • create short simple texts on paper and on screen • write chronological and non-chronological texts using simple structures
B	2	• draw on knowledge and experience of texts in deciding and planning what and how to write • sustain form in narrative and maintain consistency in non-narrative • make adventurous word and language choices appropriate to the style and purpose of the text • select from different presentational features to suit particular writing purposes • use planning to establish clear sections for writing • use appropriate language to make sections hang together
C	3	• make decisions about form and purpose, identify success criteria and use them to evaluate writing • use beginning, middle and end to write narratives in which events are sequenced logically and conflicts resolved • write non-narrative texts using structures of different text types • select and use a range of technical and descriptive vocabulary • signal sequence, place and time to give coherence and group related material into paragraphs
D	4	• develop and refine ideas in writing using planning and problem-solving strategies • use settings and characterisation • write convincing and informative non-narrative texts • organise text into paragraphs to distinguish between different information, events or processes
E	5	• reflect independently and critically on their own writing and edit and improve it • experiment with different narrative forms and styles to write their own stories • adapt non-narrative forms and styles to write fiction or factual texts • experiment with the order of sections and paragraphs to achieve different effects
F	6	• use different narrative techniques to engage and entertain the reader • in non-narrative, establish, balance and maintain viewpoints • select words and language drawing on their knowledge of literary features and formal and informal writing • use varied structures to shape and organise text coherently
G	6 Extension	• independently write and present a text with the reader and purpose in mind • use a range of narrative devices to involve the reader • add persuasive emphasis to key points • organise ideas into a coherent sequence of paragraphs

Curriculum links

Northern Ireland
Language and Literacy – Writing

Book	Year	Objectives
A	2	• observe the teacher modelling specific writing strategies • use stories as models for structuring their own writing • write in a range of genres with teacher guidance • begin to show evidence of sequence in recount and instructions
B & C	3 & 4	• participate in modelled and independent writing • talk about and plan what they are going to write • begin to check their work in relation to specific criteria • write for a variety of purposes and audiences • express thoughts and opinions in imaginative and factual writing
D–G	5–7 Extension	• participate in modelled and independent writing • discuss various features of layout in texts and apply these, as appropriate, within their own writing • write for a variety of purposes and audiences, selecting, planning and using appropriate style and form • use the skills of planning, revising and redrafting to improve their writing • express thoughts and opinions in imaginative and factual writing • begin to formulate their own personal style

Wales
English – Writing

Book	Year	Objectives
A & B	1 & 2	• organise and present imaginative and factual writing in different ways, helpful to the purpose, task and reader and incorporating some of the different characteristics of forms that are used • plan and review their writing, assembling and developing their ideas and presenting their writing clearly • write with increasing confidence, fluency and accuracy • write in a range of genres, incorporating some of the different characteristics of these forms
C–G	3–6 Extension	• use the characteristic features of literary and non-literary texts in their own writing, adapting their style to suit the audience and purpose • draft and improve their work and present writing appropriately • write for a range of purposes, for a range of real or imagined audiences, in a range of forms and in response to a range of stimuli

Curriculum links

Republic of Ireland
English Language – Writing

Book	Class	Objectives
A	Senior Infants	• receive help from the teacher, who will sometimes act as a scribe • write frequently, write for different audiences and see writing displayed • see the teacher model writing as an enjoyable experience • write about everyday experience or about something just learned • write stories
B & C	1st/2nd Class	• experience a classroom environment that encourages writing • observe the teacher as he/she models writing stories • experience how a story structure is organised by reading and listening to fiction • write regularly for different audiences, explore different genres and have writing valued • experience an abundance of oral language activity when preparing a writing task • realise that first attempts at writing are not necessarily the finished product and learn to undertake second drafts in order to improve writing • write in a variety of genres, write about something that has been learned, write the significant details about an event or an activity, write an explanation for something and write stories
D & E	3rd/4th Class	• experience a classroom environment that encourages writing • observe the teacher modelling different writing genres • use reading as a stimulus to writing • write stories that explore a variety of genres • receive and give positive responses to writing and see his/her writing valued • experience varied and consistent oral language activity as a preparation for writing • learn to use questions as a mechanism for expanding and developing a story • give sequence to ideas and events in stories • develop an appreciation of how the intended audience should influence the nature of a piece of writing • learn to revise and redraft writing • write in a variety of genres with greater sophistication • write down directions on how to perform a particular process and create stories
F & G	5th/6th Class	• experience a classroom environment that encourages writing • observe the teacher model a wide variety of writing genres • experience interesting and relevant writing challenges • receive and give constructive responses to writing and see his/her writing valued • experience a level of success in writing that will be an incentive to continue writing • experience varied and consistent oral language activity as part of the pre-writing process • observe the teacher improving writing • write independently through a process of drafting, revising, editing and publishing • choose a register of language and presentation appropriate to subject and audience • write in a variety of genres and write for a particular purpose and audience • argue the case in writing for a particular point of view • write stories

Prim-Ed Publishing   www.prim-ed.com
PRIMARY WRITING

Curriculum links

Book	Level	Objectives
A–C	First	• enjoy exploring and discussing text structures • appreciate the richness of language and texts • write independently, use appropriate punctuation and order sentences in a way that makes sense • check writing makes sense throughout the writing process • present writing in a way that will make it legible and attractive for the reader • use notes and other types of writing to help create new text • consider the type of text being created and select ideas and information, organise these in a logical sequence and use interesting words • convey information, describe events or processes, share opinions and persuade the reader in different ways • explore the elements writers use in different genres and use this to compose stories with interesting structures, characters and/or settings
C–F	Second	• enjoy exploring and discussing text structures • appreciate the richness of language and texts • use appropriate punctuation, vary sentence structures and divide work into paragraphs • check writing makes sense and meets its purpose throughout the writing process • consider the impact that layout and presentation have • use notes and other types of writing to create new text • consider the type of text being created and select ideas and information, organise these in an appropriate way for the purpose and use suitable vocabulary for the audience • use language and style to engage and/or influence the reader • convey information, describe events and explain processes in different ways • persuade, argue, explore issues or express an opinion using relevant supporting detail and/or evidence • write for different purposes and readers • explore the elements writers use in different genres and use this to compose stories with an interesting and appropriate structure, interesting characters and/or settings which come to life
F–G	Third	• enjoy exploring and discussing increasingly complex texts and structures • appreciate the influence texts can have • punctuate and structure different types of sentences and arrange these into paragraphs • review and edit writing to ensure it meets its purpose and communicates meaning throughout the writing process • consider the impact that layout and presentation will have on the reader • use notes and other types of writing to create original text • consider the type of text being created and select ideas and information, organise these in an appropriate way for the purpose and use suitable vocabulary for the audience • engage and/or influence readers through use of language, style and tone as appropriate to the genre • convey information, describe events and explain processes or concepts • persuade, argue, evaluate, explore issues or express an opinion, using a clear line of thought and relevant supporting detail and/or evidence • explore the elements writers use and compose texts in different genres, using some of the conventions of chosen genre successfully and/or creating convincing narratives, characters and settings

Structural and language features are shown on the left and right of the text below.

Title	Cup final hero!	
Orientation – who, when, where, why	Richard Riggs and Brian Bowen arrived early at Paul Peckham's house. This was the day the trio had dreamt of all season. Their football team, Robe Rockets, were in the final of the Northern Districts Cup to be held at the local park. The boys had attended every training session, played in every match and, among them, had scored most of the goals. But even Richard and Brian had to agree, Paul Peckham was the **star player**.	• varied and interesting adjectives; e.g. **lucky, magic**
Complication and significant events – in detail	Paul packed his **lucky** boots in his bag. He had worn them for every match this season and had scored 47 goals. He was hoping to reach the **magic** 50 with a hat-trick today. With Paul's dog Romelyn at their heels, the boys set off for the park. As they passed the end of the main street, a shout and a loud whizzing noise made them turn quickly. Before he realised what was happening, Paul was knocked to the ground and, as he fell, his bag was dragged from his arm. In a second, the **assailant** was gone. 'After him! Quickly! He's got my boots!' Paul cried in despair, as he staggered up. The boys ran after him but were no match for a thief on a skateboard. Romelyn, however, was up for the chase. Tearing down pathways, jumping over walls and squeezing through fences, the fit dog was enjoying a great workout. The boy on the board had not expected a pursuer with such dogged determination! He climbed a tree in an effort to escape, **but** Romelyn was on his scent and found him immediately.	• appropriate paragraphing • descriptive language; e.g. **star player, assailant** • a range of conjunctions to connect text; e.g. **but, and**
Resolution – to the complication	The three boys followed the sound of familiar barking and waited at the base of the tree, while the boy sheepishly climbed down. 'Sorry', he mumbled. 'I was just having a laugh.' 'Well, we need someone to look after Romelyn while we play our match **and** I think he's decided that someone is you', declared Paul. 'Come on, or we'll be late!' In the closing minutes of what had been a nail-biting match, the score was level at two all. Paul's lucky boots kicked two goals. A foul from the opposing team gave Robe Rockets a penalty and a chance for the Cup, and for Paul Peckham, the chance of reaching the magic 50. The spectators hushed as he prepared to take his kick. Just as his foot made contact with the ball, Romelyn barked wildly. Time stood still. Would the ball find the back of the net?	• verbs in the past tense; e.g. **blew, was carried**
Conclusion – indicating what has changed	The referee **blew** the whistle for the end of the match, the tournament and the season. The crowd went berserk. Paul Peckham **was carried** at shoulder height by his team. 'Robe Rockets are the champions', screamed the voice through the loud hailer. 'Three cheers for the champions and the lucky boots of Paul Peckham! Hip hip …!'	

Teacher information

- Discuss what a narrative is and explain that it can be presented in many forms; e.g. poem, myth, fairytale.
- Read and discuss the narrative on page 3 with the pupils.
- Discuss the different sections and explain that a framework gives the narrative order and helps the reader to understand the story.
- Identify the language features outlined to the right of the text above and work through the analysis on page 4 with the pupils.
- Plan a similar narrative, writing ideas for each section within the framework and discuss and model how the plan is transformed into a coherent piece of text.
- Pupils use page 5 to plan and then write a story of an incident centred around a sport in which they might take part.
- Pupils categorise their work based on the sport involved. A class book can then be produced, with stories arranged by sport. (Context)
- This book can be made available to pupils from other classes. (Publishing/Purpose/Audience)

- Pupils work can be displayed against a background of illustrations appropriate to each sport. (Display)

Answers

Page 4

1. Teacher check
2. (a) They love football. They are dedicated team players. They are skilful football players.
   (b) The match was held at the end of the season at the park.
3. A boy on his skateboard knocked Paul Peckham to the ground and stole his bag containing his lucky boots.
4. (a) Romelyn, by chasing and catching the assailant.
   (b) Looking after Romelyn during the match.
5. (a) The Robe Rockets won the Cup. Paul Peckham scored a hat-trick (three goals) and achieved the magic 50.
   (b) Teacher check

Cup final hero!

Richard Riggs and Brian Bowen arrived early at Paul Peckham's house. This was the day the trio had dreamt of all season. Their football team, Robe Rockets, were in the final of the Northern Districts Cup, to be held at the local park. The boys had attended every training session, played in every match and, among them, had scored most of the goals. But even Richard and Brian had to agree, Paul Peckham was the star player.

Paul packed his lucky boots in his bag. He had worn them for every match this season and had scored 47 goals. He was hoping to reach the magic 50 with a hat-trick today. With Paul's dog Romelyn at their heels, the boys set off for the park.

As they passed the end of the main street, a shout and a loud whizzing noise made them turn quickly. Before he realised what was happening, Paul was knocked to the ground and, as he fell, his bag was dragged from his arm. In a second, the assailant was gone.

'After him! Quickly! He's got my boots!' Paul cried in despair, as he staggered up.

The boys ran after him but were no match for a thief on a skateboard. Romelyn, however, was up for the chase.

Tearing down pathways, jumping over walls and squeezing through fences, the fit dog was enjoying a great workout. The boy on the board had not expected a pursuer with such dogged determination! He climbed a tree in an effort to escape, but Romelyn was on his scent and found him immediately.

The three boys followed the sound of familiar barking and waited at the base of the tree, while the boy sheepishly climbed down.

'Sorry', he mumbled. 'I was just having a laugh.'

'Well, we need someone to look after Romelyn while we play our match and I think he's decided that someone is you', declared Paul. 'Come on, or we'll be late!'

In the closing minutes of what had been a nail-biting match, the score was level at two all. Paul's lucky boots had kicked two goals. A foul from the opposing team gave Robe Rockets a penalty and a chance for the Cup, and for Paul Peckham, the chance of reaching the magic 50. The spectators hushed as he prepared to take his kick. Just as his foot made contact with the ball, Romelyn barked wildly. Time stood still. Would the ball find the back of the net?

The referee blew the whistle for the end of the match, the tournament and the season. The crowd went berserk. Paul Peckham was carried at shoulder height by his team.

'Robe Rockets are the champions', screamed the voice through the loud hailer. 'Three cheers for the champions and the lucky boots of Paul Peckham! Hip hip … !'

Use the narrative on page 3 to complete the page.

1. Title

Give reasons for both Paul Peckham and Romelyn being a 'Cup final hero'.

Paul Peckham	Romelyn

2. Orientation

(a) What are you told about the main characters?

_____

_____

_____

(b) When and where does the Cup final match take place?

_____

3. Complication and events

Briefly describe the problem and how it happened.

_____

_____

_____

_____

_____

4. Resolution

(a) Who solved the problem and how? _____

_____

(b) How did the assailant pay for his deed? _____

_____

5. Conclusion

(a) What are the three main points of the conclusion?

_____

_____

_____

(b) Write an addition to the conclusion about the boy on the skateboard.

_____

_____

1. Plan a narrative based on a sports story.

Title

Orientation

Complication and events

Resolution

Conclusion

2. Write your narrative.

3. Edit your work.

Structural and language features are shown on the left and right of the text below.

Title	Shipwreck!	
Orientation – who, when, where, why	Ian rushed to the kitchen, still struggling to pull his jumper over his head. He grabbed a piece of cold toast and smothered it with a layer of honey. Picking up his **bulging** school bag, he yelled goodbye to his mum and flew through the front door, but he was too late. He gazed in despair **as** the bus disappeared around the corner. Muttering to himself, Ian began his trek to school.	• varied and interesting adjectives; e.g. **bulging, unexpected**
Complication and significant events – in detail	As he turned the corner into the main street, an **unexpected** wind almost knocked him off his feet. He could taste the salty air on his lips. What was going on? Before him lay a cliff path, and beside it, a sheer drop to the sea below, **pounding relentlessly** against the shore. Screams rang out, mingling with the sounds of the wind and ocean. 'What the ...?' Ian looked over the cliff. People were in the water, fully clothed, battling against the angry swell. Some were dragging chests up the beach, **while** others carried lifeless bodies to the sanctuary of the shallow caves. It was then he noticed their clothes were from a bygone age. He looked out to sea and saw a ship. Its masts had been broken like matchsticks by the raging tempest. The hull was being **smashed mercilessly** on the rocks. He saw the ship break up and watched as it gradually sank beneath the waves. Someone had salvaged the ship's nameplate. Ian could just make out the name, *Dolphin*. He shouted to the people below, but his small voice was carried away on the wind. 'I must get help!' he cried.	• appropriate paragraphing • a range of conjunctions to connect text; e.g. **as, while** • descriptive language; e.g. **pounding relentlessly, smashed mercilessly**
Resolution – to the complication	As he turned to run, he tripped over his bag and fell. Picking himself up, he saw the familiar landmarks of the main street. There was no wind, no cliff path, no crashing sea. Dazed and confused, Ian **continued** on his way to school.	• verbs in the past tense; e.g. **continued, gasped**
Conclusion – indicating what has changed	'Delighted you could join us, Ian', sneered Mr James over the top of his half-moon spectacles. 'Quickly now, Chapter 5 of *European history.*' Ian rummaged noisily through his desk and pulled out the book, turning quickly to the correct page. He **gasped**. He couldn't believe his eyes. The title of the chapter was, *The wreck of the* Dolphin.	

Teacher information

- Discuss what a narrative is and explain that it may be presented in many forms; e.g. poem, play, legend, imaginative story.
- Read and discuss the narrative on page 7 with the pupils.
- Discuss the different sections and explain that a framework gives the narrative order and helps the reader to understand the story.
- Identify the language features listed above and work through the analysis on page 8 with the pupils.
- Plan a similar narrative, writing ideas for each section within the framework and discuss and model how the plan is transformed into a coherent piece of text.
- Pupils use page 9 to plan and then write an imaginative narrative with a historical twist.
- Pupils' work can be published, illustrated and displayed on a time line, determined by the approximate date of the twist in their stories. (Publishing/Display)
- Pupils read their stories in an authors' circle. (Purpose/ Audience)
- Within the authors' circle, pupils choose a story to dramatise for the rest of the class. (Purpose)

Answers

Page 8

1. Teacher check

2. (a) Ian

   (b) Possible answers – He didn't want to:

      (i) miss the bus   (ii) walk to school

      (iii) be late for school

   (c) (i) in the morning   (ii) Ian is going to school

3. (a) Ian has a time warp experience.

   (b) Turning the corner into the main street

   (c) People dragging chests on to the beach; carrying bodies into caves; a ship being wrecked, breaking up and finally sinking

4. As Ian trips and falls over his bag, everything returns to normal.

5. At school, the class are studying the shipwreck Ian has just witnessed.

Shipwreck!

Ian rushed to the kitchen, still struggling to pull his jumper over his head. He grabbed a piece of cold toast and smothered it with a layer of honey. Picking up his bulging school bag, he yelled goodbye to his mum and flew through the front door, but he was too late. He gazed in despair as the bus disappeared around the corner. Muttering to himself, Ian began his trek to school.

As he turned the corner into the main street, an unexpected wind almost knocked him off his feet. He could taste the salty air on his lips. What was going on? Before him lay a cliff path, and beside it, a sheer drop to the sea below, pounding relentlessly against the shore. Screams rang out, mingling with the sounds of the wind and ocean.

'What the …?'

Ian looked over the cliff. People were in the water, fully clothed, battling against the angry swell. Some were dragging chests up the beach, while others carried lifeless bodies to the sanctuary of the shallow caves. It was then he noticed their clothes were from a bygone age. He looked out to sea and saw a ship. Its

masts had been broken like matchsticks by the raging tempest. The hull was being smashed mercilessly on the rocks. He saw the ship break up and watched as it gradually sank beneath the waves. Someone had salvaged the ship's nameplate. Ian could just make out the name, *Dolphin*. He shouted to the people below, but his small voice was carried away on the wind.

'I must get help!' he cried.

As he turned to run, he tripped over his bag and fell. Picking himself up, he saw the familiar landmarks of the main street. There was no wind, no cliff path, no crashing sea. Dazed and confused, Ian continued on his way to school.

'Delighted you could join us, Ian', sneered Mr James over the top of his half-moon spectacles. 'Quickly now, Chapter 5 of *European history*.'

Ian rummaged noisily through his desk and pulled out the book, turning quickly to the correct page. He gasped. He couldn't believe his eyes. The title of the chapter was, *The wreck of the* Dolphin.

Use the narrative on page 7 to complete the page.

1. Title

Give the story a more
interesting title.

2. Orientation

(a)   Who is the main character of the story? _____

(b)   Write three possible reasons why he was rushing.

  (i)   _____

  (ii) _____

  (iii) _____

(b)   (i)   When does the story take place? _____

  (ii) Explain how you know this. _____

  _____

3. Complication and events

(a)   What happens to Ian as he walks to
school?

  _____

  _____

(b)   Where is he when it occurs?

  _____

  _____

(c)   What does Ian witness during the
complication?

  _____

  _____

  _____

  _____

4. Resolution

How is the problem resolved?

5. Conclusion

What is the twist to the
story?

1. Plan a narrative for an imaginative story with a historical twist.

Title

Orientation

Complication and events

Resolution

Conclusion

2. Write your narrative.

3. Edit your work.

Structural and language features are shown on the left and right of the text below.

Title	A midnight visit
Orientation – who, when, where, why	Something had woken Georgia from a deep sleep. Through the window, she noticed a **twinkling** light at the bottom of the garden. Quietly, she slipped out of the house to investigate. What greeted her when she tiptoed behind the shed was the **most amazing sight** she had ever seen.
Complication and significant events – in detail	Three strange-looking creatures were deep in conversation, looking at a flying saucer with what appeared to be a broken wing. 'Can I help you?' she inquired softly. 'My name's Georgia. I live here.' The creatures jumped in surprise, **but** seemed comforted by her friendly voice. 'We are Zoloots from the planet Zolootia', the tallest one announced. 'Our craft has a malfunction. We must repair it before we can return home.'
Resolution – to the complication	'No problem! Dad's got all the latest power tools. Friends call him Power Tool Pete!' Georgia opened the door to the shed. The Zoloots gasped. 'It's like stepping back in time! We've only seen relics like this in a museum! Do they still work?' questioned the spectacled Zoloot in amazement. 'I should think so', huffed Georgia. 'They are the best you can get!' The Zoloots studied the tools carefully **before** choosing one to fix the problem. In no time at all, the job was done and they were ready to leave. 'Is there anything else you need?' offered Georgia. 'Some of those plants would be nice', answered the **spectacled** Zoloot, pointing to a very overgrown patch of garden. 'Dad would be delighted if you took all of those', laughed Georgia. 'They're all weeds. Mum's been nagging him for ages to get rid of them.' With a **sweep of their arms**, the Zoloots lifted every last weed. 'Magic!' laughed Georgia. 'But how will I explain this to Dad?'
Conclusion – indicating what has changed	Back in her room, Georgia **pondered** how she could prove the Zoloots had really been here. 'Of course! The weeds!' she cried. She ran out into the night. There was all the proof she needed. What had earlier been an overgrown patch of garden, full of weeds, was now a magnificent display of exotic flowering plants. 'Well, now I really have got some explaining to do!' she **giggled**, skipping back into the house.

- varied and interesting adjectives; e.g. **twinkling, spectacled**

- appropriate paragraphing

- a range of conjunctions to connect text; e.g. **but, before**

- descriptive language; e.g. **most amazing sight, sweep of their arms**

- verbs in the past tense; e.g. **pondered, giggled**

Teacher information

- Discuss what a narrative is and explain that it may be presented in many forms; e.g. poem, play, legend, imaginative story.
- Read and discuss the narrative on page 11 with the pupils.
- Discuss the different sections and explain that a framework gives the narrative order and helps the reader to understand the story.
- Work through the analysis on page 12 with the pupils.
- Plan a similar narrative, writing ideas for each section within the framework and discuss and model how the plan is transformed into a coherent piece of text.
- Pupils use page 13 to plan and then write an imaginative science fiction narrative.
- Pupils publish and illustrate their work before sorting it into three groups, based on reading levels. The work can then be bound into three volumes which can be read to other classes. (Publishing/Purpose/Audience)
- In groups, pupils can read stories written by others. (Purpose/Audience)

Answers

Page 12
1. Teacher check
2. Who? – Georgia

   Where? – at the bottom of Georgia's garden

   When? – in the middle of the night

   What? – a twinkling light at the bottom of the garden
3. The Zoloots' spacecraft had broken down and they needed to make repairs before they could return home.
4. Georgia allowed them to use tools from her father's shed. They fixed their craft and left, weeding the garden as they went.
5. Teacher check

A midnight visit

Something had woken Georgia from a deep sleep. Through the window, she noticed a twinkling light at the bottom of the garden. Quietly, she slipped out of the house to investigate. What greeted her when she tiptoed behind the shed was the most amazing sight she had ever seen.

Three strange-looking creatures were deep in conversation, looking at a flying saucer with what appeared to be a broken wing.

'Can I help you?' she inquired softly. 'My name's Georgia. I live here.'

The creatures jumped in surprise, but seemed comforted by her friendly voice.

'We are Zoloots from the planet Zolootia', the tallest one announced. 'Our craft has a malfunction. We must repair it before we can return home.'

'No problem! Dad's got all the latest power tools. Friends call him Power Tool Pete!'

Georgia opened the door to the shed. The Zoloots gasped.

'It's like stepping back in time! We've only seen relics like this in a museum! Do they still work?' questioned the spectacled Zoloot in amazement.

'I should think so', huffed Georgia. 'They are the best you can get!'

The Zoloots studied the tools carefully before choosing one to fix the problem. In no time at all, the job was done and they were ready to leave.

'Is there anything else you need?' offered Georgia.

'Some of those plants would be nice', answered the spectacled Zoloot, pointing to a very overgrown patch of garden.

'Dad would be delighted if you took all of those', laughed Georgia. 'They're all weeds. Mum's been nagging him for ages to get rid of them.'

With a sweep of their arms, the Zoloots lifted every last weed.

'Magic!' laughed Georgia. 'But how will I explain this to Dad?'

Back in her room, Georgia pondered how she could prove the Zoloots had really been here.

'Of course! The weeds!' she cried.

She ran out into the night. There was all the proof she needed. What had earlier been an overgrown patch of garden, full of weeds, was now a magnificent display of exotic flowering plants.

'Well, now I really have got some explaining to do!' she giggled, skipping back into the house.

Examining narrative ③

Use the narrative on page 11 to complete the page.

1. Title

Which title, do you think, best fits the text? Tick your choice.

☐ Zoloots meet an alien

☐ Strange meeting at midnight

☐ Gardeners from another planet

2. Orientation

What does the first paragraph tell us?

Who?

Where?

When?

What?

3. Complication and events

Write a brief description of the complication with the spacecraft.

_____

_____

_____

_____

4. Resolution

Write a brief description of the resolution.

_____

_____

_____

_____

5. Conclusion

Write a different ending to the story.

_____

_____

_____

1. Plan a narrative for an imaginative science fiction story.

Title

Orientation

Complication and events

Resolution

Conclusion

2. Write your narrative.

3. Edit your work.

Structural and language features are shown on the left and right of the text below.

Title	**Steve Waugh – Australian cricket legend**
Orientation – who, when, where, why	Steve Waugh was born in Sydney, Australia, in June 1965. **As a youngster**, he was a keen football player, with his sights set firmly on a career in that sport. But **at the age of 17**, Steve was spotted by a cricket talent scout. This encounter led to his glittering future with the bat and ball.
Events – in detail	In 1985, wearing the baggy green cap for the first time, Steve played for Australia on a tour of South Africa. During his successful, 19-year career, he played in 168 test matches for Australia, scoring a total of 10 927 runs and producing many memorable performances. The most notable of these included his 200 against the West Indies in 1995, his twin centuries against England in 1997 and his 120 against South Africa in the 1999 World Cup. He is one of only two players to have been on the winning side for Australia in two World Cup finals, in 1987 against England and in 1999 against Pakistan. In 1999, he became the 40th captain of the Australian Test Team, holding this office until his retirement from the game in 2004.
	After a tour in India, Steve became actively involved in the development of the Udayan Home in Barrackpore. At the home, children exposed to leprosy, an infectious disease affecting the skin and respiratory system, are provided with health care, an education and opportunities for a brighter future.
	Back in Australia, Steve devoted time to the young people at the Spastic Centre of New South Wales and supported children with cancer in his role as patron of Camp Quality.
	As he loves to travel, Steve was lucky that his career **took** him to many places around the world. He **has written** several books about cricket and life on tour. He has become Australia's best-selling sports author.
	Since retiring from international cricket, Steve has been involved in plans to create a Cricket City in India. The project would include a cricket academy, schools, accommodation and lifestyle and leisure opportunities.
Conclusion – indicating value of event	In recognition for his contribution to cricket and the wider community, Steve Waugh was voted Australian of the Year in 2004. He is respected and admired throughout the world and will continue to be an inspiration to sports fans for many years to come.

- appropriate paragraphing

- vocabulary to suggest passing of time; e.g. **As a youngster, at the age of 17**

- verbs in the past tense; e.g. **took, has written**

Teacher information

- Discuss what a recount is, explaining that a biography is only one example.
- Read and discuss the recount on page 15 with the pupils.
- Discuss the different sections of the framework and ensure pupils understand how the text fits into each one.
- Emphasise the language features listed to the right of the text above.
- Work through the analysis on page 16 with the pupils.
- Plan a similar recount, writing ideas for each section within the framework and discuss and model how the plan is transformed into a coherent piece of text.
- Pupils use page 17 to plan and then write a recount in the form of a biography.
- Pupils glue their work on to an A3-sized page, surrounding it with pictures of their chosen personality. (Display)
- Pupils read their biographies to the class, briefly explaining reasons for their choice. (Purpose/Audience)
- Pupils categorise their subjects based on careers; e.g. sports heroes, TV and film personalities, politicians. A class book can then be produced.(Context)
- This book can be made available to pupils from other classes. (Publishing/Purpose/Audience)

Answers

Page 16
1. Teacher check
2. (1) Waugh (2) cricketer (3) Sydney/Australia
   (4) football (5) 17
3. (a) Teacher check
   (b) Answers will vary but may include information on his family, hobbies, favourite music etc.
   (c) To portray an image of the whole person and not just one aspect of his life.
4. Teacher check

Steve Waugh
Australian cricket legend

Steve Waugh was born in Sydney, Australia, in June 1965. As a youngster, he was a keen football player, with his sights set firmly on a career in that sport. But at the age of 17, Steve was spotted by a cricket talent scout. This encounter led to his glittering future with the bat and ball.

In 1985, wearing the baggy green cap for the first time, Steve played for Australia on a tour of South Africa. During his successful, 19-year career, he played in 168 test matches for Australia, scoring a total of 10 927 runs and producing many memorable performances. The most notable of these included his 200 against the West Indies in 1995, his twin centuries against England in 1997 and his 120 against South Africa in the 1999 World Cup. He is one of only two players to have been on the winning side for Australia in two World Cup finals, in 1987 against England and in 1999 against Pakistan. In 1999, he became the 40th captain of the Australian Test Team, holding this office until his retirement from the game in 2004.

After a tour in India, Steve became actively involved in the development of the Udayan Home in Barrackpore. At the home, children exposed to leprosy, an infectious disease affecting the skin and respiratory system, are provided with health care, an education and opportunities for a brighter future.

Back in Australia, Steve devoted time to the young people at the Spastic Centre of New South Wales and supported children with cancer in his role as patron of Camp Quality.

As he loves to travel, Steve was lucky that his career took him to many places around the world. He has written several books about cricket and life on tour. He has become Australia's best-selling sports author.

Since retiring from international cricket, Steve has been involved in plans to create a Cricket City in India. The project would include a cricket academy, schools, accommodation and lifestyle and leisure opportunities.

In recognition for his contribution to cricket and the wider community, Steve Waugh was voted Australian of the Year in 2004. He is respected and admired throughout the world and will continue to be an inspiration to sports fans for many years to come.

Examining recount 1

Use the recount on page 15 to complete the page.

1. Title

Suggest two alternative titles for the text.

2. Orientation

Complete the paragraph.

Steve _____¹, a famous Australian _____,² was born

in _____³. He wanted to be a professional _____⁴

player but was chosen to play cricket at the age of _____⁵.

3. Events

(a) Make a list of six topics about which a biographer could write.

(b) What other information do you think people might want to know about Steve Waugh?

(c) Why do you think it is necessary to include information about things other than cricket in Steve Waugh's biography?

4. Conclusion

Write an alternative conclusion to this recount.

1. Plan a recount in the form of a biography.

Title

Orientation

Events

Conclusion

2. Write your biography.

3. Edit your work.

Structural and language features are shown on the left and right of the text below.

Title	THE SUNDAY REPORTER 20 MARCH 1932	
	SYDNEY HARBOUR BRIDGE OPENS	• appropriate paragraphing
Orientation – who, when, where, why	Yesterday's eagerly anticipated opening of Sydney Harbour Bridge was disrupted by confusion and delay, as the ceremony ribbon was cut unexpectedly by an interloper searching for a moment of glory.	
Events – in order, with detail	**While** an estimated crowd of 750 000 or more filled the streets of the city, looking forward to a day of entertainment and celebration, Captain Francis De Groot of the New Guard was stealing the limelight, high above the harbour on the newly completed bridge.	• vocabulary to suggest passing of time; e.g. **While, until**
	De Groot gained access to the official area by disguising himself as a member of the Governor's cavalry guard. Dressed in full uniform, he rode at the rear of the procession **until** it reached the ceremony area. With a loud cry, he charged forward, and, raising his sword high in the air, slashed the ribbon. He reportedly cried out that he did so on behalf of decent and loyal citizens of New South Wales and declared the bridge open. The excited captain was quickly arrested and later charged with antisocial behaviour.	• verbs in the past tense; e.g. **continued, were allowed**
	The ribbon was hastily retied by red-faced officials. Using jewel encrusted scissors, the formal opening by New South Wales Premier, Mr Jack Lang, proceeded without further upset. A message from Tottenham Primary School 550 kilometres away, delivered by relays of children, was presented to the Premier on the bridge. A 21-gun salute and Royal Australian Air Force fly-past added to the splendour of the occasion, informing everyone within earshot that the bridge was now officially open.	
	The festival atmosphere **continued** for the remainder of the day, as people **were allowed** to walk on the roadway amid a vast display of floats and marching bands.	
Conclusion – indicating value of event	This impressive feat of engineering now stands high above the waters of Sydney's magnificent harbour for all to see and use. To commemorate yesterday's historic occasion, three postage stamps have been issued.	

Teacher information

- Discuss what a recount is, explaining that this newspaper report is about an important civic event.
- Read and discuss the recount on page 19 with the pupils.
- Discuss the different sections of the framework and ensure pupils understand how the text fits into each one.
- Emphasise the language features listed to the right of the text above.
- Pupils complete the analysis on page 20.
- Plan a similar recount, writing ideas for each section within the framework and discuss and model how the plan is transformed into a coherent piece of text.
- Pupils use page 21 to plan and then write a recount in the form of a newspaper report.
- Pupils present their work as a class newspaper, giving each story an appropriate eye-catching title and illustration. A copy of the publication could be printed for other classes. (Publishing/Purpose/Audience)
- A montage of photographs and pictures could be made to highlight a display of pupils' work. (Display)

Answers

Page 20
1. Teacher check
2. main: opening of the bridge
   secondary: De Groot's disruption
3. main features:
   Paragraph 2: De Groot gained access to official area dressed in uniform, riding on horseback. He charged forward and slashed the ribbon. He was arrested.
   Paragraph 3: The ribbon was retied. The formal opening took place. The message from Tottenham Primary School was received. There was a 21-gun salute followed by a RAAF fly-past.
   rewrite: Teacher check
4. Teacher check

20 MARCH 1932

STHE SUNDAY REPORTER

SYDNEY HARBOUR BRIDGE OPENS

Yesterday's eagerly anticipated opening of Sydney Harbour Bridge was disrupted by confusion and delay, as the ceremony ribbon was cut unexpectedly by an interloper searching for a moment of glory.

While an estimated crowd of 750 000 or more filled the streets of the city, looking forward to a day of entertainment and celebration, Captain Francis De Groot of the New Guard was stealing the limelight, high above the harbour on the newly completed bridge.

De Groot gained access to the official area by disguising himself as a member of the Governor's cavalry guard. Dressed in full uniform, he rode at the rear of the procession until it reached the ceremony area. With a loud cry, he charged forward, and, raising his sword high in the air, slashed the ribbon. He reportedly cried out that he did so on behalf of decent and loyal citizens of New South Wales and declared the bridge open. The excited captain was quickly arrested and later charged with antisocial behaviour.

The ribbon was hastily retied by red-faced officials. Using jewel encrusted scissors, the formal opening by New South Wales Premier, Mr Jack Lang, proceeded without further upset. A message from Tottenham Primary School 550 kilometres away, delivered by relays of children, was presented to the Premier on the bridge. A 21-gun salute and Royal Australian Air Force fly-past added to the splendour of the occasion, informing everyone within earshot that the bridge was now officially open.

The festival atmosphere continued for the remainder of the day, as people were allowed to walk on the roadway amid a vast display of floats and marching bands.

This impressive feat of engineering now stands high above the waters of Sydney's magnificent harbour for all to see and use. To commemorate yesterday's historic occasion, three postage stamps have been issued.

Use the recount on page 19 to complete the page.

1. Title

Write an appropriate eye-catching title for this newspaper report.

2. Orientation

This recount introduces two incidents, one main and one secondary.
What are they?

main	secondary

3. Events

Write notes about the main features of paragraphs 2 and 3 in the events section, then rewrite them in your own words.

	main features	rewrite
2		
3		

4. Conclusion

Write a new conclusion for the recount.

1. Plan a recount in the form of a newspaper report.

Title

Orientation

Events

Conclusion

2. Write your recount.   **3.** Edit your work.

Structural and language features are shown on the left and right of the text below.

Title	**Jump!**
Orientation – who, when, where, why	The day dawned crisp and clear. It was going to be a 'scorcher', but I could not think beyond the events of the advancing morning. I had just three goals. Get ready. Climb in. Jump out. I could see the aircraft taxiing towards the hangar, preparing to take six flightless beings, of which I was one, 1000 metres above the ground before ejecting us, unceremoniously, into the cool atmosphere.
Events – in order, with detail	We had been drilled over and over, covering every possible solution to every possible problem—except the one to which there was no solution! But on this score, we had been assured that every silk had been professionally folded and the chances of one not opening were less than negligible.
	I donned my overalls and laced my sturdy boots, ready now to strap on my harness and secure my helmet. Our instructor was giving last minute advice. I didn't want to listen. It would confuse me. I wanted to go out and get it over with.
	At the allotted time, we were summoned by the pilot, a jovial man with a wicked glint in his eye. We crossed to the plane in single file. There was an atmosphere of 'fighter pilot' in the air. I began to feel excited as we climbed on board.
	Seconds later, the engine started and we prepared for take-off. As we climbed higher, we could see how beautiful the land was, a real bird's-eye view. Just for a moment, I forgot why I was there. 'Ready?'
	I gulped. I positioned myself at the open doorway, looking into the plane and the blank faces of my comrades. Once the engine cut out, I had to go.
	I fell backwards and time stood still.
	'I've forgotten to count!' I shrieked to no-one. '... four elephants, five elephants, six elephants. Check canopy!'
	As I descended, the cold air **slapped** my face and the wind screamed in my ears. I could see many familiar landmarks on the patchwork landscape. I felt like a celestial lord, guarding my kingdom. What an exhilarating experience!
	Using the straps on the harness, I **guided** myself into the wind to reduce my speed. As the ground rushed up to meet me, I had to remember the drills for a controlled landing. Feet and knees together. Bend legs. Fall sideways.
Conclusion – indicating value of event	It was over all too quickly. As I lay on the ground, unharmed, all I could think of was how soon I could do it again! But I hadn't quite finished. I jumped up and waved wildly to the control tower, letting them know I was okay.

Right-side annotations:
- appropriate paragraphing
- vocabulary to suggest passing of time; e.g. **At the allotted time, Seconds later**
- verbs in the past tense; e.g. **slapped, guided**

Teacher information

- Discuss what a recount is, explaining that it can be presented in many different forms.
- Read and discuss the recount on page 23 with the pupils.
- Discuss the different sections of the framework and ensure pupils understand how the text fits into each one.
- Emphasise the language features listed to the right of the text above.
- Pupils complete the analysis on page 24.
- Plan a similar recount, writing ideas for each section of the framework and discuss and model how the plan is transformed into a coherent piece of text.
- Pupils use page 25 to plan and then write a recount in the form of an exciting personal experience.
- Pupils present their recounts, either handwritten or as computer print-outs, to another class to read. (Publishing/ Purpose/Audience)
- Pupils design a background for their text. For example, the design for *Jump!* could be a coloured parachute. (Display)

Answers

Page 24

1. Teacher check

2. (a) Answers may include: climb in, jump out, flightless beings, ejecting us, cool atmosphere
   (b) Who, how, what, when, where
   (c) Teacher check

3. (a) the training
   (b) getting dressed and last minute advice
   (c) climbing aboard
   (d) flying to altitude
   (e) jumping out
   (f) descending

4. (a) The writer felt exhilarated and wanted to do it again, very soon.
   (b) Initially, the writer was very apprehensive.

JUMP!

The day dawned crisp and clear. It was going to be a 'scorcher', but I could not think beyond the events of the advancing morning. I had just three goals. Get ready. Climb in. Jump out. I could see the aircraft taxiing towards the hangar, preparing to take six flightless beings, of which I was one, 1000 metres above the ground before ejecting us, unceremoniously, into the cool atmosphere.

We had been drilled over and over, covering every possible solution to every possible problem—except the one to which there was no solution! But on this score, we had been assured that every silk had been professionally folded and the chances of one not opening were less than negligible.

I donned my overalls and laced my sturdy boots, ready now to strap on my harness and secure my helmet. Our instructor was giving last minute advice. I didn't want to listen. It would confuse me. I wanted to go out and get it over with.

At the allotted time, we were summoned by the pilot, a jovial man with a wicked glint in his eye. We crossed to the plane in single file. There was an atmosphere of 'fighter pilot' in the air. I began to feel excited as we climbed on board.

Seconds later, the engine started and we prepared for take-off. As we climbed higher, we could see how beautiful the land was, a real bird's-eye view. Just for a moment, I forgot why I was there.
'Ready?'
I gulped. I positioned myself at the open doorway, looking into the plane and the blank faces of my comrades. Once the engine cut out, I had to go.

I fell backwards and time stood still. 'I've forgotten to count!' I shrieked to no-one. '... four elephants, five elephants, six elephants. Check canopy!'

As I descended, the cold air slapped my face and the wind screamed in my ears. I could see many familiar landmarks on the patchwork landscape. I felt like a celestial lord, guarding my kingdom. What an exhilarating experience!

Using the straps on the harness, I guided myself into the wind to reduce my speed. As the ground rushed up to meet me, I had to remember the drills for a controlled landing. Feet and knees together. Bend legs. Fall sideways.

It was over all too quickly. As I lay on the ground, unharmed, all I could think of was how soon I could do it again! But I hadn't quite finished. I jumped up and waved wildly to the control tower, letting them know I was okay.

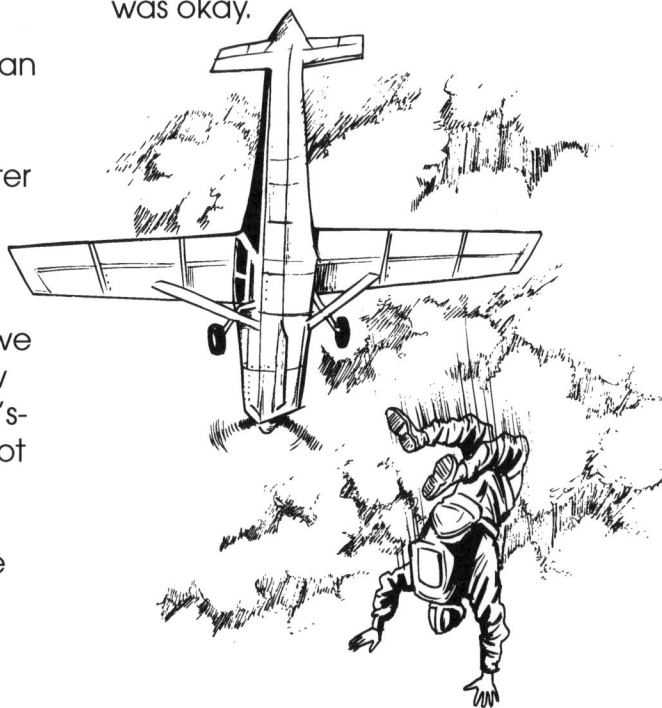

Use the recount on page 23 to complete the page.

1. Title

(a) Write four words to describe how would you feel about doing a parachute jump.

_____

_____

(b) Give the text a new title, based on your feelings.

2. Orientation

(a) Which words indicate that the text is about a parachute jump?

(b) Circle the five questions answered in the paragraph.

Who?   How?

What?   When?

Where?   Why?

(c) Write an extra sentence to answer the question not included.

Question: _____

Answer: _____

_____

_____

3. Events

Six events are described before the writer actually landed. Write them in order.

(a) _____   (b) _____

(c) _____   (d) _____

(e) _____   (f) _____

4. Conclusion

(a) Explain how the writer felt about the parachute jump.

_____

_____

_____

(b) How does this differ from the writer's feelings at the beginning of the recount?

_____

_____

_____

1. Plan a recount of an exciting personal experience.

Title

Orientation

Events

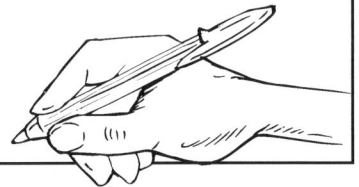

Conclusion

2. Write your recount.   **3.** Edit your work.

Structural and language features are shown on the left and right of the text below.

Title	**Apple and cinnamon toasties**
Goal – the purpose of the procedure	Recipe will make four apple and cinnamon toasties (toasted sandwiches).
Materials – the materials required to complete the procedure	**Ingredients** • 8 slices bread (try sultana bread for more flavour!) • 2 large green apples • butter or margarine • **125 g ricotta cheese** • 2 tablespoons currants • 1/4 teaspoon cinnamon **Equipment** • toasted sandwich maker • **butter knife** • measuring spoons • peeler • grater • wooden spoon • bowl • cooking spray (non-stick)
Method – clear steps in a logical order	**Method** 1. Turn on sandwich maker to begin heating. 2. **Peel and grate apples.** 3. Place grated apple, currants, ricotta cheese and cinnamon in bowl. 4. **Stir ingredients well.** 5. Spray surface of sandwich maker with cooking spray (lightly). 6. Butter two slices of bread. Place in sandwich maker with buttered side down. 7. Use wooden spoon to place apple mixture in centre of bread. Too much mixture will mean toastie will not seal around edges. 8. Butter two more slices of bread. 9. **Cover** apple mixture with bread, buttered side up. 10. Close sandwich maker and **toast** for three minutes or until golden brown. 11. Repeat steps 6–10 to make two more toasties.
Test – an evaluation	Test apple and cinnamon toasties by tasting them. (Allow a minute or two for filling to cool down first!)

Right-hand notes:

• subject-specific vocabulary; e.g. **125 g ricotta cheese, butter knife**

• clear concise information—unnecessary words omitted; e.g. **Peel and grate apples, Stir ingredients well**

• the present tense is used; e.g. **Cover, toast**

Teacher information

• Collect a variety of recipe books. Distribute to pupils in small groups and give them the task of finding the 'structure' of a recipe. Groups report back to the class.

• Read the text on page 27 with the class. The text can be enlarged using the accompanying CD on an interactive whiteboard. Discuss each section of the procedure.

• Focus on the language of the text. Note that unnecessary words (such as 'the') are omitted. The steps are written simply and clearly and are easy to follow.

• The first word of each step in the method of this procedure begins with a directing verb—these types of verbs are called 'command' verbs. Ask pupils for more examples of command verbs (imperatives).

• Discuss which tense is being used in the procedure and ask for pupils to give examples of this.

• Work through the analysis on page 28 with the class.

• Before pupils attempt to plan and write their procedure, using the plan on page 29, model this process to the class. Write a procedure for a simple recipe such as scrambled egg on toast.

Procedure 1 plan – possible ingredients for toasties include cheese, ham, pineapple, tomatoes, baked beans, fruit, honey and other spreads.

• Once the pupils' recipes have been planned and written, they should be proofread and edited. Pupils can publish their recipes using a word processor. Collate the recipes to make a class recipe book. (Publishing/Purpose/Audience)

• Choose a recipe to follow and make during a cooking lesson. (Purpose/Context)

• Use a digital camera to take photographs of each step of the recipe being made. Enlarge the procedure for the recipe to A3 size and attach the photographs to each step. Discuss sequencing with the class. (Display/Publishing/Context)

• If funds are available for the ingredients, pupils can make their own toastie recipes. Hold a 'tastiest toastie' competition or, alternatively, sell the toasties to other pupils as a class fund raiser. (Purpose/Audience)

Answers

Page 28

1. Apple and cinnamon

2. 4

3. (a) The materials come before the method so the reader can collect the items required before beginning the procedure.

 (b) The ingredients are the edible materials and the equipment is the utensils and appliances—the non-edible materials.

4. (a) • Place grated apple, currants, ricotta cheese and cinnamon in bowl. (3)

 • Stir ingredients well. (4)

 • Peel and grate apples. (2)

 • Spray surface of sandwich maker with cooking spray (lightly). (5)

 • Turn on sandwich maker to begin heating. (1)

 (b) The steps are numbered to show the reader they must be followed in order.

 (c) Teacher check

5. Test apple and cinnamon toasties by tasting them, but allow a minute or two for the filling to cool down first.

Apple and cinnamon toasties

Recipe will make four apple and cinnamon toasties (toasted sandwiches).

Ingredients..
- 8 slices bread (try sultana bread for more flavour)
- 2 large green apples
- butter or margarine
- 125 g ricotta cheese
- 2 tablespoons currants
- $\frac{1}{4}$ teaspoon cinnamon

Equipment..
- toasted sandwich maker
- butter knife
- measuring spoons
- peeler
- grater
- wooden spoon
- bowl
- cooking spray (non-stick)

Method..
1. Turn on sandwich maker to begin heating.
2. Peel and grate apples.
3. Place grated apple, currants, ricotta cheese and cinnamon in bowl.
4. Stir ingredients well.
5. Spray surface of sandwich maker with cooking spray (lightly).
6. Butter two slices of bread. Place in sandwich maker with buttered side down.
7. Use wooden spoon to place apple mixture in centre of bread. Too much mixture will mean toastie will not seal around edges.
8. Butter two more slices of bread.
9. Cover apple mixture with bread, buttered side up.
10. Close sandwich maker and toast for three minutes or until golden brown.
11. Repeat steps 6–10 to make two more toasties.

Test apple and cinnamon toasties by tasting them. (Allow a minute or two for filling to cool down first!)

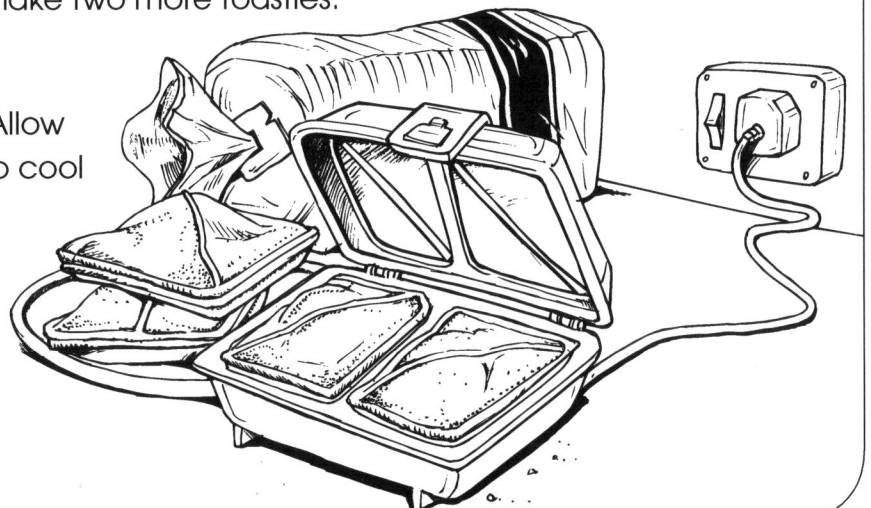

Use the procedure on page 27 to complete the page.

1. Title

The recipe is for which type of toasties?

2. Goal

The goal of the recipe is to make

2   4   6   8

apple and cinnamon toasted sandwiches.

3. Ingredients

(a)   Why are the materials listed before the method?

_____

_____

(b)   Explain why there are two lists in this section of the procedure.

_____

_____

4. Method

(a)   Write the number of each step in the box.

☐ Place grated apple, currants, ricotta cheese and cinnamon in bowl.

☐ Stir ingredients well.

☐ Peel and grate apples.

☐ Spray surface of sandwich maker with cooking spray (lightly).

☐ Turn on sandwich maker to begin heating.

(b)   Why are the steps in the method numbered?

_____

_____

(c)   Do you think diagrams showing each step of the procedure would be useful? Colour a rating on the scale.

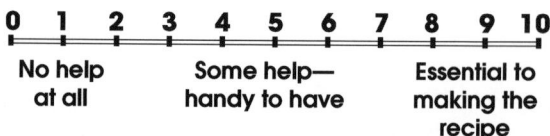

0 1 2 3 4 5 6 7 8 9 10

No help at all   Some help— handy to have   Essential to making the recipe

5. Test

How and when can you test if the recipe is a success?

1. Plan a procedure for a recipe you know well or for a different type of toastie. (Toasties can be savoury or sweet.)

Title

Goal

Ingredients

Equipment

Method

Numbered steps in order.

Test

How will you test if your recipe works?

2. Write your procedure.

3. Edit your work.

Structural and language features are shown on the left and right of the text below.

Title		
	How many drops?	• subject-specific vocabulary; e.g. **eye-dropper, Record estimate**
Goal – the purpose of the procedure	Aim: To find out how many drops of water will fit on a small coin.	
Materials – the materials required to complete the procedure	Materials: • **small coin** • detergent • **eye-dropper** • toothpick • water • newspaper • jar or cup	• clear concise information—unnecessary words omitted; e.g. **small coin, Half-fill jar with water**
Method – clear steps in a logical order	Method: 1. Place newspaper on desk. 2. **Half-fill jar with water**. 3. Practise using eye-dropper. Suction water in and drop back into jar—one drop at a time. 4. Estimate how many drops of water will fit on coin. **Record estimate**. 5. Drop individual droplets of water on coin from very low height. Count each drop. Continue until no more drops will fit on coin. How many drops? 6. **Repeat** Step 5 a number of times. Does the number of drops change? 7. When maximum number of droplets are balancing on coin (just before water spills over edge), **bend** down to height of desktop and look at shape of water on coin. 8. Dip toothpick into detergent and **touch** bubble of water. What happens? 9. **Add** small amount of detergent to water in jar. Repeat Step 5. What difference does detergent make to results?	• the present tense is used; e.g. **touch, Add** • command verbs used in instructions; e.g. **Repeat, bend**
Results (Test) – an evaluation	Results: Water droplets form bubble-shaped dome on coin. When touched with soapy toothpick, bubble breaks. Water mixed with detergent does not hold together as strongly, so water spreads out over the coin.	

Teacher information

• Ask the class to think about science experiments they have conducted. What is included in a science experiment procedure? Explain to the class that an experiment is written similarly to a recipe, but some sections have different names; for example, the 'ingredients' are called 'materials'.

• Read the text on page 31 with the class. The text can be enlarged using the accompanying CD on an interactive whiteboard. Discuss each section of the procedure with the class.

• Focus on the language of the text. Note that unnecessary words (such as 'the') are omitted. The steps are written simply and clearly and are easy to follow.

• One word (often the first) of each step in the method is a directing verb—these types of verbs are called 'command' verbs. Ask pupils for more examples of command verbs (imperatives).

• Discuss which tense is being used in the procedure and ask for pupils to give examples of this.

• Work through the analysis on page 32 with the class.

• Before pupils attempt to plan and write their procedure, using the plan on page 33, model this process to the class by planning a procedure for a simple science experiment, such as testing which materials are attracted to a magnet.

• Show the class how to use the plan to write the procedure. It is important the class understands that a plan does not contain every word of the written text—just the main points.

• Procedure 2 plan is an activity to investigate how different materials absorb water. For pupils who need guidance, materials to be tested could include: tissue paper, newspaper, magazine paper, aluminium foil, writing paper, paper towel etc. Discuss making the procedure a 'fair test', by measuring and using the same amount of water each time.

• Pupils plan, write and edit their procedures.

• Display the science experiments for all pupils to read. Choose one and demonstrate it to the class. Offer the author suggestions for improvements. (Display/Audience/Purpose)

• Gather the materials required for the pupils to conduct their own experiments. Record their investigations using a digital camera. Display the photographs with the procedures. Pupils can give their experiments a rating and present their suggestions for improvements to the class. (Purpose/Publishing/Display)

Answers

Page 32

1. How many drops?

2. ... drops of water will fit onto a small coin.

3. (a) 7
   (b) Answers will vary. Possible answer: So they can be read quickly and easily.

4. (a) • Half-fill jar with water. (2)
       • Place newspaper on desk. (1)
       • Repeat step 5 a number of times. Does the number of drops change? (6)
       • Dip toothpick into detergent and touch bubble of water. What happens? (8)
   (b) If the steps are not followed in the correct order, the procedure will not work.
   (c) capital, letter, full, stop, command

5. (a) Scientific diagrams are drawn as accurately as possible and all parts are labelled.
   (b) Answers will vary

How many drops?

Aim: To find out how many drops of water will fit on a small coin.

Materials:

- small coin
- detergent
- eye-dropper
- newspaper
- jar or cup
- toothpick
- water

Method:

1. Place newspaper on desk.
2. Half-fill jar with water.
3. Practise using eye-dropper. Suction water in and drop back into jar—one drop at a time.
4. Estimate how many drops of water will fit on coin. Record estimate.
5. Drop individual droplets of water on coin from very low height. Count each drop. Continue until no more drops will fit on coin. How many drops?
6. Repeat Step 5 a number of times. Does the number of drops change?
7. When maximum number of droplets are balancing on coin (just before water spills over edge), bend down to height of desktop and look at shape of water on coin.
8. Dip toothpick into detergent and touch bubble of water. What happens?
9. Add small amount of detergent to water in jar. Repeat Step 5. What difference does detergent make to results?

Results:

Water droplets form bubble-shaped dome on coin.

When touched with soapy toothpick, bubble breaks.

Water mixed with detergent does not hold together as strongly, so water spreads out over the coin.

Surface tension is a force that pulls together molecules on the surface of a liquid, making it act like a skin.

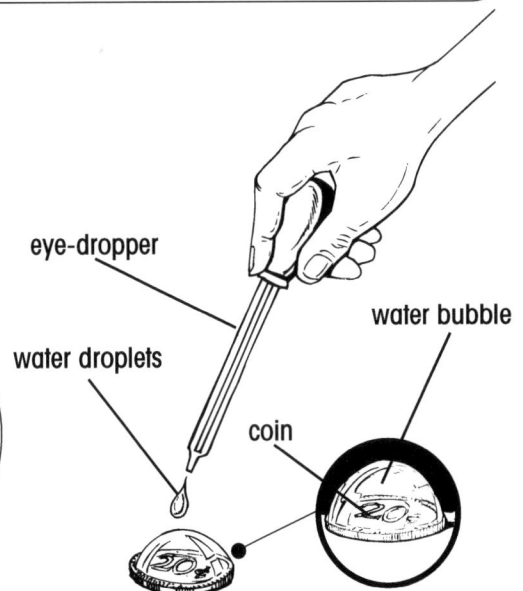

eye-dropper

water bubble

water droplets

coin

Use the procedure on page 31 to complete the page.

1. Title

Write the title of the procedure in the box, using interesting lettering and colour.

2. Aim

The aim of the procedure is to find out how many _____

_____

3. Materials

(a) How many materials are required to complete the procedure? _____

(b) Why are the materials set out as a list using bullet points?

_____

4. Method

(a) Write the number of each step in the box.

☐ Half-fill jar with water.	☐ Place newspaper on desk.
☐ Repeat Step 5 a number of times. Does the number of drops change?	☐ Dip toothpick into detergent and touch bubble of water. What happens?

(b) Explain why the order of the steps is important. _____

_____

(c) Add the missing words to the sentences.

Each step of the method begins with a c_____

l_____ and ends in a f_____ s_____.

The first word of most steps is a c_____ verb.

5. Test

(a) A scientific diagram is included in the results. How is it different from a picture?

(b) If you were to complete this science procedure, would the diagram be useful? Explain.

1. Plan a science procedure to investigate how well different materials absorb water.

Title

Aim

Materials

Method

Numbered steps in order.

Results

How should the results be recorded?

2. Write your procedure.

3. Edit your work.

Structural and language features are shown on the left and right of the text below.

Title	**The chocolate game**	• subject-specific vocabulary; e.g. **knife and fork(s)**, **clockwise** or **anti-clockwise**
Goal – the purpose of the procedure	Goal: To roll a six and eat as many squares of chocolate as possible!	
Materials – the materials required to complete the procedure	You will need: • family block of chocolate • **knife and fork(s)** • a placemat • 1 die • 'dress-up' clothes such as hat, scarf and gloves	• clear concise information—unnecessary words omitted; e.g. **Put placemat in centre of circle, First player rolls die.**
Method – clear steps in a logical order	What to do: 1. Organise players into circle. 2. **Put placemat in centre** of circle. Open bar of chocolate and place on mat with knife and fork. 3. **Place** dress-up clothes in centre of circle. 4. **Decide** who starts game. (Players roll die—highest number begins game.) 5. Decide which direction die will travel—**clockwise or anti-clockwise**. 6. **First player rolls die**. If six is rolled, player enters circle and puts on dress-up clothes. Player uses knife and fork to cut one square of chocolate at a time and eat it. 7. Next player rolls die. If number other than six is rolled, that player passes die to next person in circle, who tries to roll a six. 8. Once a six is rolled, the player in middle of circle **stops** eating chocolate, **removes** dress-up clothes and returns to spot in circle. 9. The player who rolled six enters circle, puts on dress-up clothes and eats chocolate with knife and fork. 10. Continue game until all chocolate has been eaten.	• command verbs used in instructions; e.g. **Place, Decide** • the present tense is used; e.g. **stops, removes**
Test – an evaluation	The winner is the person who eats the most chocolate.	

Teacher information

- Ask pupils to think of games they have played, using the instructions to help them with the rules. (For example, board games.) What is usually included in these instructions?

- Read the text on page 35 with the class. The text can be enlarged using the accompanying CD on an interactive whiteboard. Discuss each section of the procedure with the class.

- Focus on the language of the text. Note that unnecessary words (such as 'the') are omitted. The steps are written simply and clearly and are easy to follow.

- The first word of some steps in the method is a directing verb—these types of verbs are called 'command' verbs. Ask pupils for more examples of command verbs (imperatives).

- Discuss the tense used in the procedure and point out examples of words in the present tense.

- Work through the analysis on page 36 with the class.

- Before pupils attempt to plan and write their procedure, using the plan on page 37, model this process to the class by planning a procedure for another simple party game, such as 'Musical chairs'.

- Show the class how to use the plan to write the procedure. It is important to stress that a plan does not contain every word of the written text—just the main points.

  Before pupils begin writing, they may like to use the Internet or resource centre to find lists of children's party games. Ask pupils of different nationalities to share the games they play at parties, to see if they are different from those on the list.

- Pupils plan, write and edit their procedures.

- Pupils can publish their procedures using a word processor or neat handwriting. Artwork can be included. The party games can be collated to form a class book of games. (Publishing/Display)

- Pupils can give their party game procedure to a group in the class to play. The group must follow the instructions precisely. The players offer feedback to the author with suggestions for making the instructions clearer. (Audience/ Purpose)

- Organise to 'buddy' with a younger class. Pupils collect the materials required for the games and organise groups of younger pupils to play them. Take photographs of the pupils with a digital camera and attach them to the class book of party games. (Audience/Purpose/Publishing)

Answers

Page 36
1. Teacher check
2. To roll a six and eat as many squares of chocolate as possible.
3. (a) ... the reader needs to collect the items required before beginning the procedure.
   (b) If an item is left off the materials list, the reader will be unable to play the game.
4. (a) Method
   (b) (i) Organise, Put, Place, Decide
       (ii) command verbs
   (c) Put dress-up clothes in centre of circle.
5. The winner needs to roll sixes and eat the most chocolate.

The chocolate game

Goal: To roll a six and eat as many squares of chocolate as possible!

You will need:

- family block of chocolate
- a placemat
- knife and fork(s)
- die
- 'dress-up' clothes such as a hat, scarf and gloves

What to do:

1. Organise players into circle.

2. Put placemat in centre of circle. Open bar of chocolate and place on mat with knife and fork.

3. Place dress-up clothes in centre of circle.

4. Decide who starts game. (Players roll die—highest number begins game.)

5. Decide which direction die will travel—clockwise or anti-clockwise.

6. First player rolls die. If six is rolled, player enters circle and puts on dress-up clothes. Player uses knife and fork to cut one square of chocolate at a time and eat it.

7. Next player rolls die. If number other than six is rolled, that player passes die to next person in circle, who tries to roll a six.

8. Once a six is rolled, the player in middle of circle stops eating chocolate, removes dress-up clothes and returns to spot in circle.

9. The player who rolled six enters circle, puts on dress-up clothes and eats chocolate with knife and fork.

10. Continue game until all chocolate has been eaten.

The winner is the person who eats the most chocolate.

Examining procedure 3

Use the procedure on page 35 to complete the page.

1. Title

Write an alternative title for this game.

2. Goal

What is the goal of the procedure?

_____

_____

3. Materials

(a) Finish the sentence.

The materials are listed before the method because ...

_____

_____

(b) What would happen if something needed was left off the list of materials?

_____

_____

4. Method

(a) Another name for the section called 'What to do' is the _____.

(b) (i) List the first word of Steps 1.–4. in 'What to do'. (Remember capital letters.)

(ii) What are these types of verbs called? _____ verbs

(c) Procedures are written clearly so they can be easily followed. Unnecessary words are not included. Rewrite this passage after crossing out all unnecessary words.

Pick up all of their dress-up clothes. When you have done this put all of the dress-up clothes right in the centre of the circle that the children were organised into.

_____

_____

5. Test

What does the winner need to do?

_____

1. Plan a procedure for playing a party game such as 'Pass the parcel', 'Musical statues', 'Pin the tail on the donkey' or your own choice.

Title

Goal

Materials

What you need.

Method

Numbered steps in order.

Test

How will you know who won the game?

2. Write your procedure.   **3.** Edit your work.

Structural and language features are shown on the left and right of the text below.

Title	**Wildlife wonderland**	
Classification – a general statement about the subject of the report	Kakadu National Park, located in Australia's tropical north, is indeed a wildlife wonderland. The variety of flora and fauna found in the park **is** extremely large and it is this variety that **attracts** thousands of visitors to Kakadu each year.	• written in timeless present tense; e.g. **is**, **attracts**
Description – provides accurate description and facts	**Kakadu** can be found in the far north of the Northern Territory from the coast to the Arnhem Land plateau, covering an area of 20 000 square kilometres. **The park** gets **its** name from an Aboriginal Australian floodplain language, 'Gagudju', which was one of the regular languages spoken in northern Kakadu.	• written in the third person; e.g. **Kakadu, The park, its**
	Kakadu is home to the **longest continuing human culture** in the world. Aboriginal people have lived in the Kakadu region for more than 40 000 years. Rock paintings can be found in the Kakadu region in over 5000 locations and contain some of the earliest known storytelling art in the world. Evidence of the oldest types of **edge-ground axes** has also been found.	• uses factual language rather than imaginative; e.g. **longest continuing human culture**
	The park has two seasons: the 'wet' (November to April) and the 'dry' (May to October). However, the Aboriginal people of Kakadu recognise six seasons. The best time to visit Kakadu is during the dry season when all the tracks are accessible.	
	Three major rivers flow through Kakadu: Wildman River, West Alligator River and the huge South Alligator River. Almost the entire catchment area of the South Alligator River is in Kakadu. Other diverse environments include a sandstone plateau and escarpment, monsoon rainforests, savannah, woodlands, floodplains, waterfalls, mangroves and **mudflats**.	• information is organised into paragraphs
	Kakadu has an amazing range of flora and fauna. There are approximately 1700 plant species, 60 species of native mammals, 280 kinds of birds, 120 kinds of reptiles, 10 000 types of insects, 25 different frogs and 53 different species of freshwater fish.	• technical vocabulary and subject-specific terms are used; e.g. **edge-ground axes, mudflats**
Conclusion – final comment about the subject of the report. (It includes a personal comment by the writer.)	Kakadu National Park is jointly managed by its traditional Aboriginal owners and the Australian government's Department of the Environment and Heritage. It is World Heritage listed for both its natural and cultural heritage. After visiting Kakadu, it is easy to see why it is considered one of the most fascinating wildlife and cultural reserves in the world.	

Teacher information

• Read through the information report with the pupils and discuss the features of a report.

• Work through the analysis on page 40 with the class.

Explain that: 'I', 'we', 'my' and 'our' are examples of the first person

'you' and 'your' are examples of the second person

'he', 'she', 'it' and 'they' are examples of the third person

For example: **I** swam in the river. (first person)

You swam in the river. (second person)

Lachlan swam in the river./**They** swam in the river. (third person)

• Before pupils attempt to plan and write their own information report, model this process with the whole class, choosing a place of interest pupils have studied in class or are familiar with.

• Pupils should use page 41 to plan and write their own information report. They will need to have gathered sufficient information about the place of their choice prior to planning their report.

• Pupils' reports could be read out orally by them in small groups or to the whole class, and then discussed. (Purpose/Audience)

• Published reports, accompanied with appropriate illustrations or photographs, could be displayed for other pupils to read and compare. (Publishing/Display/Purpose)

• The activity could be done in conjunction with a geography topic. (Context/Purpose)

Answers

Page 40

1. (a) Wildlife wonderland

(b) Teacher check

2. Teacher check

3. (a) 5

(b) Paragraph 1 of the description

(c) Teacher check

(d) Answers may include sandstone plateau and escarpment, monsoon rainforests, savannah, woodlands, floodplains, waterfalls or mangroves

(e) is, are

(f) Aboriginal people have lived in the Kakadu region for more than 40 000 years.

4. The writer agrees it is easy to see why Kakadu is considered one of the most fascinating wildlife and cultural reserves in the world.

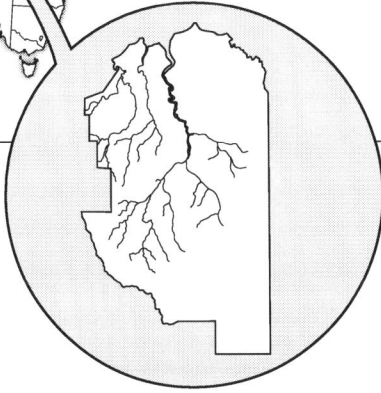

Wildlife wonderland

Kakadu National Park, located in Australia's tropical north, is indeed a wildlife wonderland. The variety of flora and fauna found in the park is extremely large and it is this variety that attracts thousands of visitors to Kakadu each year.

Kakadu can be found in the far north of the Northern Territory from the coast to the Arnhem Land plateau, covering an area of 20 000 square kilometres. The park gets its name from an Aboriginal Australian floodplain language, 'Gagudju', which was one of the regular languages spoken in northern Kakadu.

Kakadu is home to the longest continuing human culture in the world. Aboriginal people have lived in the Kakadu region for more than 40 000 years. Rock paintings can be found in the Kakadu region in over 5000 locations and contain some of the earliest known storytelling art in the world. Evidence of the oldest types of edge-ground axes has also been found.

The park has two seasons: the 'wet' (November to April) and the 'dry' (May to October). However, the Aboriginal people of Kakadu recognise six seasons. The best time to visit Kakadu is during the dry season when all the tracks are accessible.

Three major rivers flow through Kakadu: Wildman River, West Alligator River and the huge South Alligator River. Almost the entire catchment area of the South Alligator River is in Kakadu. Other diverse environments include a sandstone plateau and escarpment, monsoon rainforests, savannah, woodlands, floodplains, waterfalls, mangroves and mudflats.

Kakadu has an amazing range of flora and fauna. There are approximately 1700 plant species, 60 species of native mammals, 280 kinds of birds, 120 kinds of reptiles, 10 000 types of insects, 25 different frogs and 53 different species of freshwater fish.

Kakadu National Park is jointly managed by its traditional Aboriginal owners and the Australian government's Department of the Environment and Heritage. It is World Heritage listed for both its natural and cultural heritage. After visiting Kakadu, it is easy to see why it is considered one of the most fascinating wildlife and cultural reserves in the world.

Use the report on page 39 to complete the page.

1. Title

(a) The title of this information report is

_____

(b) Why do you think this title was chosen?

_____

_____

2. Classification

List two facts from this section of the report.

_____

_____

3. Description

(a) How many paragraphs make up the description section?

(b) Which paragraph in this section explains how the park got its name?

(c) An example of factual language is 'the longest continuing human culture'. List another example of factual language from the report.

_____

(d) List three more technical words that describe the diverse environments found in Kakadu.

mudflats

(e) Circle the present tense verbs in this sentence.

The best time for tourists to visit Kakadu is during the dry season when all the tracks are accessible.

(f) Replace one word with 'Aboriginal people' to change this sentence from the first to the third person.

We have lived in the Kakadu region for more than 40 000 years.

_____

_____

_____

4. Conclusion

What is the writer's opinion of Kakadu?

_____

_____

1. Plan an information report about a place you have visited, have learnt about or research one you would like to visit. Remember to include accurate facts, use the present tense and to write in the third person; e.g. it, they.

Title

Classification

A general statement about the subject.

Description

Divide the description into sections. Include facts about its location, geographical features, weather, flora and fauna etc.

Conclusion

It may contain a personal opinion.

2. Write your report. 3. Edit your work.

Structural and language features are shown on the left and right of the text below.

	Terrible lizards	
Title – states what is being reported		
Classification – a general statement about the subject of the report	The word 'dinosaur' comes from a Latin word meaning 'terrible lizard'. Like lizards, dinosaurs were reptiles. They **lived over 65 million years ago** during the Mesozoic Era, the 'age of the reptiles'. Reptiles today **are related** to dinosaurs in that they both have scaly skin and lay eggs. However, it is thought that dinosaurs may be more closely related to birds.	• uses factual language rather than imaginative; e.g. **lived over 65 million years ago**
Description – provides accurate description and facts	**Dinosaurs** differed widely in areas such as size, weight, number of legs (two or four), speed of movement and what **they** ate (whether they were herbivores, carnivores or omnivores). There are two main groups of dinosaurs: (a) Saurischians or 'lizard-hipped' dinosaurs. 　This group included: 　(i) Theropods – bipedal (walked on two feet); small forelimbs, sharp teeth and claws; carnivores. Examples were Tyrannosaurus and Allosaurus. 　(ii) Sauropods – huge dinosaurs with long, heavy necks and tails; mostly quadrupedal (walked on four legs); herbivores. Examples were Apatosaurus and Diplodocus. (b) Ornithischians or 'bird-hipped' dinosaurs. 　This group included: 　(i) Plated dinosaurs – bony plates or spikes on their back or tail; small jaw; quadrupedal; herbivores. An example was Stegosaurus. 　(ii) Armoured dinosaurs – bony plates and spikes all over their body; usually a club-like tail; quadrupedal; herbivores. An example was Ankylosaurus. 　(iii) Bird-footed dinosaurs – peg-like teeth; bipedal; omnivores or herbivores. Examples were Hadrosaurus and Oviraptor. 　(iv) Horned dinosaurs – horns, beaks and large bony collars; **quadrupedal**; herbivores. Examples were **Triceratops** and Styracosaurus. Fossilised trackways show that many herbivorous dinosaurs travelled in herds, feeding and nesting together. Travelling in packs or herds offered protection against the carnivores. Some carnivores also appeared to hunt in packs to enable them to attack much larger prey.	• written in present tense; e.g. **are related** (Note: as dinosaurs are extinct, the past tense is needed in some sentences.) • written in the third person; e.g. **dinosaurs, they** • technical vocabulary and subject-specific terms are used; e.g. **quadrupedal, Triceratops**.
Conclusion – a final comment about he subject of the report. (It may include a personal comment by the writer.)	Scientists are still not sure why dinosaurs became extinct. The most popular theory is that a meteorite hit the Earth, covering it in a thick cloud of dust. This blocked the sun, and caused huge changes to the environment to which the dinosaurs were unable to adjust.	

Teacher information
- Read through the scientific report with the pupils and discuss the features of a report.
- Revise the third person. (See page 38.) Pupils complete the analysis on page 44.
- Before pupils attempt to plan and write their own scientific report, choose another animal and model this process with the whole class.
- Pupils should use page 45 to plan and write their own scientific report. They will need to have gathered sufficient information about the animal of their choice prior to planning their report.
- Pupils' reports could be read out orally by them in small groups or to the whole class, and then discussed. (Purpose/Audience)
- Published reports, accompanied with appropriate illustrations, could be displayed for other pupils to read and compare, especially those who chose the same animal or animal group. (Publishing/Display/Purpose)
- The activity could be done in conjunction with a broad or selective animal theme in science or a scientific research project. (Context/Purpose)

Answers
Page 44
1. (a) Terrible lizards
   (b) Teacher check; an acceptable answer would be: The subject is dinosaurs and the word dinosaur means 'terrible lizard'.
2. Teacher check
3. (a) (i) eats plants
   (ii) eats meat
   (iii) eats plants and meat
   (iv) a 'lizard-hipped' dinosaur
   (v) a 'bird-hipped' dinosaur
   (b) Reptiles are related to dinosaurs in that they both have scaly skin and lay eggs.
4. It discusses the most popular theory for the extinction of dinosaurs.

Terrible lizards

The word 'dinosaur' comes from a Latin word meaning 'terrible lizard'. Like lizards, dinosaurs were reptiles. They lived over 65 million years ago during the Mesozoic Era, the 'age of the reptiles'.

Reptiles today are related to dinosaurs in that they both have scaly skin and lay eggs. However, it is thought that dinosaurs may be more closely related to birds.

Dinosaurs differed widely in areas such as size, weight, number of legs (two or four), speed of movement and what they ate (whether they were herbivores, carnivores or omnivores).

There are two main groups of dinosaurs:

(a) Saurischians or 'lizard-hipped' dinosaurs.

This group included:

(i) Theropods – bipedal (walked on two feet); small forelimbs, sharp teeth and claws; carnivores. Examples were Tyrannosaurus and Allosaurus.

(ii) Sauropods – huge dinosaurs with long, heavy necks and tails; mostly quadrupedal (walked on four legs); herbivores. Examples were Apatosaurus and Diplodocus.

(b) Ornithischians or 'bird-hipped' dinosaurs.

This group included:

(i) Plated dinosaurs – bony plates or spikes on their back or tail; small jaw; quadrupedal; herbivores. An example was Stegosaurus.

(ii) Armoured dinosaurs – bony plates and spikes all over their body; usually a club-like tail; quadrupedal; herbivores. An example was Ankylosaurus.

(iii) Bird-footed dinosaurs – peg-like teeth; bipedal; omnivores or herbivores. Examples were Hadrosaurus and Oviraptor.

(iv) Horned dinosaurs – horns, beaks and large bony collars; quadrupedal; herbivores. Examples were Triceratops and Styracosaurus.

Fossilised trackways show that many herbivorous dinosaurs travelled in herds, feeding and nesting together. Travelling in packs or herds offered protection against the carnivores. Some carnivores also appeared to hunt in packs to enable them to attack much larger prey.

Scientists are still not sure why dinosaurs became extinct. The most popular theory is that a meteorite hit the Earth, covering it in a thick cloud of dust. This blocked the sun, and caused huge changes to the environment to which the dinosaurs were unable to adjust.

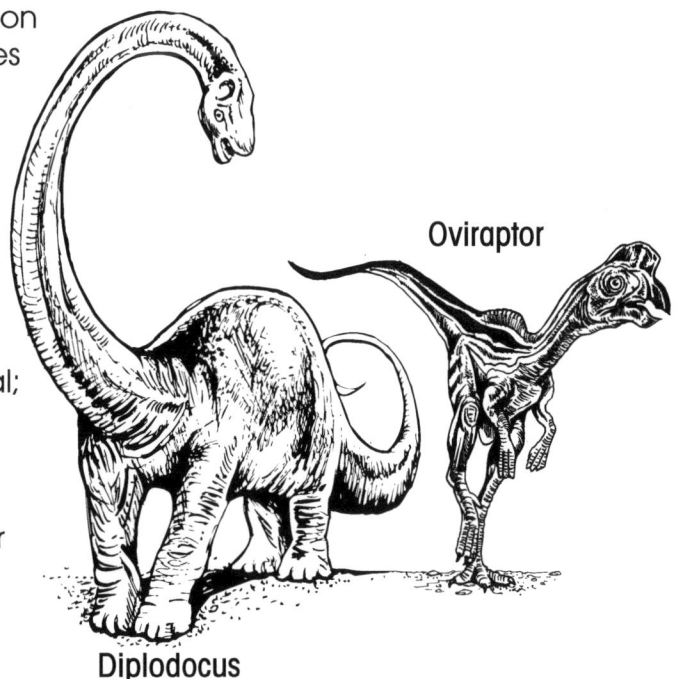

Oviraptor

Diplodocus

Use the report on page 43 to complete the page.

1. Title

(a)   The title of this scientific report is _____

(b)   Is it an appropriate title? _____   Explain why you think this.

_____

_____

2. Classification

List three facts from this section of the report.

3. Description

(a)   What do these technical words mean?

   (i)   herbivore   _____

   (iii) carnivore   _____

   (iii) omnivore   _____

   (iv) Saurischian   _____

   (v) Ornithischian _____

(b)   Replace one word with 'reptiles' and another with a pronoun such as 'he', 'she' or 'they' to change this sentence from the first to the third person.

   We are related to dinosaurs in that we both have scaly skin and lay eggs.

4. Conclusion

What is the main idea of the concluding paragraph?

_____

1. Plan a scientific report about a particular animal. Remember to use scientific vocabulary and ensure that your facts are accurate.

Title

Classification

A general statement about the subject.

Description

Divide the description into sections. Include facts about appearance, habitat, diet, behaviour etc.

Conclusion

It may contain a personal opinion.

2. Write your report.

3. Edit your work.

Structural and language features are shown on the left and right of the text below.

Structure	Text	Language features
Title – the headline states what is being reported	**The DAILY NEWS** **27 JANUARY** **FAST FOOD 'JUNKIES' ON THE INCREASE**	• uses factual language rather than imaginative; e.g. **a fast growing problem**
Classification – a sub-head or general statement about the subject of the report	Surveys in many countries around the world are showing a marked increase in the amount of junk and fast food being consumed.	
Description – provides accurate description and facts	The World Health Society has released the results of surveys from several countries including the USA, Canada, England, Australia, Germany and New Zealand, which reveal that the amount of junk food consumed is **a fast-growing problem**. Junk foods and fast foods with little nutritional value such as soft drinks, hamburgers, chips, fried chicken, biscuits and crisps are now a regular part of most people's daily diet. 'Diets **made** up of these types of foods have higher fat, sugar and salt levels', **says** World Health Society spokesperson, Carmen Fisher. 'Too much junk food could mean the body is missing out on important nutrients and can also lead to health problems such as **obesity**, heart disease, **Type 2 diabetes**, high cholesterol and tooth decay.' Ms Fisher says that the average person should eat less than 20 grams of saturated fat a day. However, just one fast food meal such as a burger and chips can contain this amount and more! The survey also shows that families are now spending up to one-third of their household budgets on junk food meals. This is usually blamed on the modern way of life with the influences of television, advertisers, and a busy, hurried lifestyle making junk and fast food an easy choice. 'A balanced diet with a variety of good food directly affects **people's** wellbeing', says Ms Fisher. 'A **person** with a healthy body sleeps well, has energy, maintains a healthy weight and generally has a happy disposition. An improper diet can have long-term ill effects on the body.'	• written in timeless present tense; e.g. **made, says** • written in the third person; e.g. **people's, person** • technical vocabulary and subject-specific terms are used; e.g. **obesity, Type 2 diabetes**
Conclusion – a final comment about the subject of the report. (It may include an expert or personal opinion, or be a summarising comment.)	Ms Fisher adds that while no-one expects adults and children to always eat healthy food, junk and fast foods should be considered treats to be eaten occasionally, rather than as regular meals. Jonathon Dodd, New York	• information is organised into paragraphs

Teacher information

• Read through the newspaper report with the pupils and discuss the features of a report. Explain how reporters follow the 'inverted pyramid' style of writing news articles, where the news item tapers from the most important detail to the least important detail; i.e. Headline, Main detail (who, what, when, where, why, how), Incidental detail

• Revise the third person. (See page 38.) Pupils complete the analysis on page 48.

• Before pupils attempt to plan and write their own newspaper report, model this process with the whole class, using another subject or issue.

• Pupils should use page 49 to plan and write their own newspaper report. They will need to have gathered information about the subject of their choice prior to planning their report.

• Pupils' reports could be read out orally by them in small groups or to the whole class, and then discussed. (Purpose/ Audience)

• Published reports, accompanied with appropriate illustrations, could be displayed for other pupils to read and compare. (Publishing/Display/Purpose)

• The activity could be done in conjunction with a health and values or geography topic. Pupils could base their report on information they have learned throughout the topic. Alternatively, it could be a report based on a school event. (Context/Purpose)

Answers

Page 48

1. (a) Fast food 'junkies' on the increase
   (b) Teacher check
2. many, world, increase, amount, consumed
3. (a) Paragraphs 2 and 5
   (b) Teacher check
   (c) Teacher check
   (d) has, maintains, sleeps, has
   (e) Families are now spending up to one-third of their household budgets on junk food meals.
4. The answer should indicate that junk food should be considered a treat and not a regular part of the diet.

The DAILY NEWS

27 January

FAST FOOD 'JUNKIES' ON THE INCREASE

Surveys in many countries around the world are showing a marked increase in the amount of junk and fast food being consumed.

The World Health Society has released the results of surveys from several countries including the USA, Canada, England, Australia, Germany and New Zealand, which reveal that the amount of junk food consumed is a fast-growing problem. Junk foods and fast foods with little nutritional value such as soft drinks, hamburgers, chips, fried chicken, biscuits and crisps are now a regular part of most people's daily diet.

'Diets made up of these types of foods have higher fat, sugar and salt levels', says World Health Society spokesperson, Carmen Fisher. 'Too much junk food could mean the body is missing out on important nutrients and can also lead to health problems such as obesity, heart disease, Type 2 diabetes, high cholesterol and tooth decay.'

Ms Fisher says that the average person should eat less than 20 grams of saturated fat a day. However, just one fast food meal such as a burger and chips can contain this amount and more!

The survey also shows that families are now spending up to one-third of their household budgets on junk food meals. This is usually blamed on the modern way of life with the influences of television, advertisers, and a busy, hurried lifestyle making junk and fast food an easy choice.

'A balanced diet with a variety of good food directly affects people's wellbeing', says Ms Fisher. 'A person with a healthy body sleeps well, has energy, maintains a healthy weight and generally has a happy disposition. An improper diet can have long-term ill effects on the body.'

Ms Fisher adds that while no-one expects adults and children to always eat healthy food, junk and fast foods should be considered treats to be eaten occasionally, rather than as regular meals.

Jonathon Dodd, New York

Use the report on page 47 to complete the page.

1. Title

(a)   The title (headline) of this newspaper report is _____

_____

(b)   Write another suitable headline. _____

_____

2. Classification

Complete the missing words from the classification.

Surveys in _____ countries around the

_____ are showing a marked _____

in the _____ of junk food being _____ .

3. Description

(a)   Which two paragraphs in the description section contain quotes from Carmen Fisher, the World Health Society spokesperson?

Paragraphs _____ and _____.

(b)   Briefly explain one fact in the first paragraph of this section.

(c)   List three more examples of technical words used in the second paragraph.

nutrients _____

_____

(d)   Circle the present tense verbs below.

| has a happy disposition |
| maintains a good weight |
| sleeps well | has energy |

(e)   Replace one word with 'families' and another with a pronoun such as; 'its', 'their' or 'they' to change this sentence from the first to the third person.

We are now spending up to one-third of our household budgets on junk food meals.

4. Conclusion

What is the main idea of the concluding paragraph?

_____

_____

1. Plan a newspaper report about a health issue. Remember to use vocabulary that is specific to your subject.

Title

A catchy headline.

Classification

A subhead or general statement about the subject of the report.

Description

Divide the description into sections. Remember to write in the third person (it, they, he etc.) and to ensure that your facts are accurate.

Conclusion

It may contain an expert or personal opinion, or be a summarising comment.

2. Write your report.

3. Edit your work.

Structural and language features are shown on the left and right of the text below.

Title	**Busy bees**	
Definition – one or more sentences that state what the explanation is about	Honey is a sweet, sticky food made by bees from nectar. It is not only enjoyed by people, it is also an important food source for bees.	• subject-specific vocabulary; e.g. **honey stomach, fructose and glucose**
Description – information presented in logical order	Bees begin making honey by visiting flowers and sucking up nectar with their long, tube-like tongues. The nectar passes into a special pouch inside the bee called its '**honey stomach**'. A bee may have to visit hundreds of flowers to fill up its honey stomach. Once it is full, the bee flies back to its hive. In the meantime, substances in the bee's honey stomach break down the complex sugar in the nectar into two simple sugars—**fructose and glucose**. These sugars are much easier for bees to digest. When the bee arrives back at its hive, it brings up the nectar and spreads it into a honeycomb cell—a hexagonal cavity made from wax. Sometimes the bee will give the nectar to another bee in the hive to do this job. **Next**, the warmth of the beehive causes the water in the nectar to evaporate, making it thicker. Sometimes bees also fan the nectar with their wings to speed up the evaporation process. **When** most of the water has evaporated, the nectar is called 'honey'. Once the honey is ready, the bees seal the cell with beeswax, which is produced in glands in their bodies. The cell remains sealed until the bees need to eat the honey.	• linking words to show cause and effect; e.g. **Next, When** • majority of verbs in simple present tense; e.g. **eat, think** • information is organised into paragraphs
Conclusion – an evaluation or interesting comment	So next time you **eat** honey, **think** about the amazing work that bees do to make it. This might help you to forget the awful fact that what you are eating was once inside a bee's stomach!	

Teacher information

• Explanations usually outline how something occurs, works or is made. This particular explanation shows how something is made.

• Members of the class could take turns to read this text aloud, or the pupils could read it independently.

• Identify the structural and language features indicated above, before the pupils complete the analysis on page 52.

• Pupils may need to use encyclopedias or other resources to plan an explanation on page 53 about using an animal or plant product. Teachers could also have the class brainstorm a list of possibilities; e.g. wool, tree sap, spices, aloe vera juice, milk etc.

• Model the planning and writing of an explanation using the framework on page 53. The pupils can then follow this example to plan and write their explanations about animal or plant products.

• Pupils could write their explanations on a large sheet of card and add three-dimensional objects relevant to their topic; e.g. a piece of wool, a papier-mâché animal etc. (Display)

• The pupils' explanations could be displayed in the school library. (Publishing/Display)

Answers

Page 52

1. Busy bees

2. Answers will vary, but should be similar to the following: Honey is a sweet, sticky food; Honey is made by bees from nectar; Honey is enjoyed by people; Honey is an important food source for bees

3. Answers should include three of the following:
   • honey stomach – a special pouch inside a bee that holds nectar
   • fructose/glucose – a simple sugar that is easy for bees to digest
   • honeycomb cell – a hexagonal cavity made from wax
   • beeswax – a substance produced in glands in a bee's body

4. Teacher check

Busy bees

Honey is a sweet, sticky food made by bees from nectar. It is not only enjoyed by people, it is also an important food source for bees.

Bees begin making honey by visiting flowers and sucking up nectar with their long, tube-like tongues. The nectar passes into a special pouch inside the bee called its 'honey stomach'. A bee may have to visit hundreds of flowers to fill up its honey stomach. Once it is full, the bee flies back to its hive.

In the meantime, substances in the bee's honey stomach break down the complex sugar in the nectar into two simple sugars—fructose and glucose. These sugars are much easier for bees to digest. When the bee arrives back at its hive, it brings up the nectar and spreads it into a honeycomb cell—a hexagonal cavity made from wax. Sometimes the bee will give the nectar to another bee in the hive to do this job.

Next, the warmth of the beehive causes the water in the nectar to evaporate, making it thicker. Sometimes bees also fan the nectar with their wings to speed up the evaporation process. When most of the water has evaporated, the nectar is called 'honey.' Once the honey is ready, the bees seal the cell with beeswax, which is produced in glands in their bodies. The cell remains sealed until the bees need to eat the honey.

So next time you eat honey, think about the amazing work that bees do to make it. This might help you to forget the awful fact that what you are eating was once inside a bee's stomach!

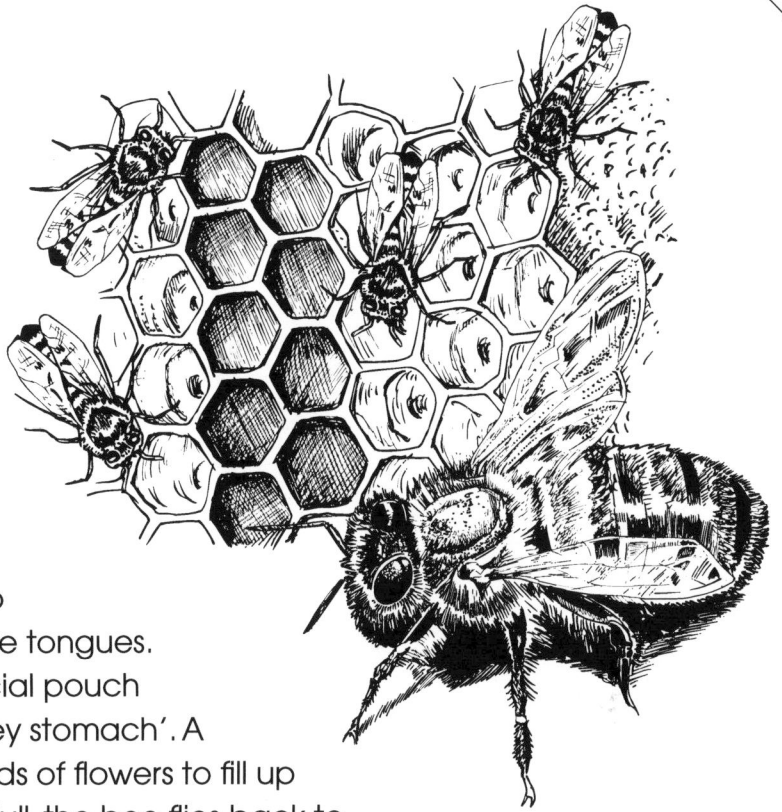

Examining explanation \ 1

Use the explanation on page 51 to complete the page.

1. Title

Write the title.

2. Definition

Imagine that someone who knew nothing about honey
read the definition. Write three simple facts they would learn.

3. Description

The paragraphs making up the description in an explanation often contain
special terms to do with the subject. Write three special terms used in the
description of this explanation and what each means.

Term	Meaning
(a)	
(b)	
(c)	

4. Conclusion

Write a new conclusion for this text that contains a different interesting
comment.

1. Plan an explanation about how we use an animal or plant product.

Title

Definition

State what the product is.

Description

Explain how we use it.

Conclusion

End with an interesting comment.

2. Write your explanation.　　　　**3.** Edit your work.

Structural and language features are shown on the left and right of the text below.

Title	**Jet engines**	
Definition – one or more sentences that state what the explanation is about	Large aircraft usually use jet engines to fly long distances at high speeds. A jet engine is one which is powered by a jet of air or gas.	• majority of verbs in simple present tense; e.g. **sucks, rises**
Description – information presented in logical order	At the front of a jet engine on a jet aircraft is a large fan, which **sucks** in air as the plane flies along. Once inside the engine, the air is 'compressed' or squeezed. This makes the pressure of the air build up. The compressed air is then mixed with jet fuel inside a special chamber and set alight. The temperature of the fuel mixture quickly **rises** to about 2000 °C—about 50 times hotter than the hottest summer's day you can imagine! **As well as** heat, the burning fuel produces gases called 'jet exhaust', which is blasted out of the back of the engine at a high speed. As the jet exhaust leaves the engine, it passes through a turbine, a set of blades attached to a shaft, which helps to drive the large fan. **Most importantly**, the action of the jet exhaust leaving the engine causes a force called 'thrust', which helps to drive the jet engine forward. Thrust is also produced by the large fan at the front of the engine. If you want to see thrust in action for yourself, try blowing up a balloon and then letting it go. You will see that the escaping air helps to drive the balloon forward, just as jet exhaust helps to drive a jet engine forward. In newer jet aircraft, only some of the air sucked into the engine is used to make **jet exhaust**. The rest passes around the engine and is added to the exhaust just as it leaves the engine. This creates even more **thrust**, keeps the engine cooler and produces less noise.	• linking words to show cause and effect; e.g. **As well as, Most importantly** • subject-specific vocabulary; e.g. **jet exhaust, thrust** • information is organised into paragraphs
Conclusion – an evaluation or interesting comment	Jet engines are likely to be around for a long time to come. Who knows what the next improvement to them will be?	

Teacher information

• Explanations usually outline how something occurs, works or is made. This particular explanation shows how something works.

• Members of the class could take turns to read this text aloud, or the pupils could read it independently.

• Identify the structural and language features indicated above, before the pupils complete the analysis on page 56.

• To assist with page 57, have the class brainstorm to create a list of imaginary machines they would like to see invented; e.g. a homework machine, a money making machine. The pupils could base their imaginary machines on real ones, in which case they may need to use encyclopedias or the Internet to research some facts.

• Model the planning and writing of an explanation using the framework on page 57. The pupils can then follow this example to plan and write their own explanation about an imaginary machine.

• Pupils should add a labelled diagram to the final copy of their explanation. (Display)

• Read aloud some of the pupils' explanations, omitting the titles and any words or phrases that give away the name of each machine. Ask the class to guess the names of the machines. Discuss which were easier to guess and why. (Purpose/Context)

Answers

Page 56

1. Teacher check

2. Answers should indicate that the definition tells us what the explanation is about.

3. (a) Answers may include the following:
   • jet exhaust – gases produced by burning jet fuel
   • turbine – a set of blades attached to a shaft
   • thrust – the force that helps to drive a jet engine forward

   (b) Answers should be similar to the following:
   1 How air is sucked into a jet engine, mixed with fuel and set alight.
   2 How jet exhaust is produced and what it does.
   3 How the engines on newer jet aircraft work differently from those on older jet aircraft.

   (c) Teacher check

4. Teacher check

JET ENGINES

Large aircraft usually use jet engines to fly long distances at high speeds. A jet engine is one which is powered by a jet of air or gas.

At the front of a jet engine on a jet aircraft is a large fan, which sucks in air as the plane flies along. Once inside the engine, the air is 'compressed' or squeezed. This makes the pressure of the air build up. The compressed air is then mixed with jet fuel inside a special chamber and set alight. The temperature of the fuel mixture quickly rises to about 2000 °C—about 50 times hotter than the hottest summer's day you can imagine!

As well as heat, the burning fuel produces gases called 'jet exhaust', which are blasted out of the back of the engine at a high speed. As the jet exhaust leaves the engine, it passes through a turbine, a set of blades attached to a shaft, which helps to drive the large fan. Most importantly, the action of the jet exhaust leaving the engine causes a force called 'thrust', which helps to drive the jet engine forward. Thrust is also produced by the large fan at the front of the engine. If you want to see thrust in action for yourself, try blowing up a balloon and then letting it go. You will see that the escaping air helps to drive the balloon forward, just as jet exhaust helps to drive a jet engine forward.

In newer jet aircraft, only some of the air sucked into the engine is used to make jet exhaust. The rest passes around the engine and is added to the exhaust just as it leaves the engine. This creates even more thrust, keeps the engine cooler and produces less noise.

Jet engines are likely to be around for a long time to come. Who knows what the next improvement to them will be?

Use the explanation on page 55 to complete the page.

1. Title

Use keywords from the text to write a new, more exciting title.

2. Definition

What is the purpose of the definition in an explanation?

3. Description

(a) Explanations often contain terms that are special to the topic. Name one special term to do with jet engines. Write its meaning.

_____   _____

                            _____

(b) Write what each paragraph in the description is about.

1 How …	**2** How …	**3** How …

(c) Most of the verbs in an explanation are in the present tense; e.g. walk, jump. List three present tense verbs used in this text.

_____   _____

4. Conclusion

The writer ends the conclusion with a question. Write another question he/she could have used instead.

_____

_____

_____

PRIMARY WRITING

Explanation plan  2

1. Plan a scientific report about how an imaginary machine works.

Title

Definition

State what the machine is.

Description

Explain what the machine does.

Conclusion

End with an interesting comment.

2. Write your explanation.   **3.** Edit your work.

Structural and language features are shown on the left and right of the text below.

Title	**Extraordinary dogs**	• subject-specific vocabulary; e.g. **breeds, 'puppy raisers'**
Definition – one or more sentences that state what the explanation is about	A guide dog is an animal that has been specially trained to act as the eyes of its visually impaired owner.	
Description – information presented in logical order	Guide dogs are usually bred by guide dog associations and are most likely to be Labrador retrievers, golden retrievers or German shepherds—**breeds** considered to have the most stable temperaments. A guide dog puppy begins its training at about eight weeks old, when it goes to live with people called '**puppy raisers**'. Puppy raisers not only house train the puppy and teach it basic obedience, they also help it to get used to riding in public transport and visiting busy places like shops. These are things a guide dog must be able to handle with ease.

When a guide dog puppy is about a year old, it is tested to see if it has the nature, intelligence and skills to be a guide dog. **If so**, it begins demanding training that lasts about three to five months.

In the first part of the training, an instructor gets the dog used to wearing a harness and handle and teaches it commands like 'forward'. One of the most difficult skills the dog must learn is to disobey an instructor's command, if following the command will lead the instructor into danger. For example, if the dog has been told to go 'forward' onto a street, but there is a car coming, it should not move. A guide dog must also learn to ignore interesting smells, noises and other animals—things that dogs naturally find irresistible!

In the second part of the training, the dog **meets** its new owner and the two begin to work together as a team. The dog also learns that whenever its harness is on, it has to work, but when it comes off, it **can behave** just like a normal dog, having fun with its owner. | • linking words to show cause and effect; e.g. **When, If so**

• majority of verbs in simple present tense; e.g. **meets, can behave**

• information is organised into paragraphs |
| **Conclusion** – an evaluation or interesting comment | Guide dogs are a vital part of life for many visually impaired people. They help to provide independence and confidence in a unique way. | |

Teacher information

• Explanations usually outline how something occurs, works or is made. This particular explanation shows how something occurs.

• Members of the class could take turns to read this text aloud, or the pupils could read it independently.

• Identify the structural and language features indicated above before the pupils complete the analysis on page 60.

• Pupils may need to use encyclopedias or other resources to plan an explanation on page 61 about training an animal. Teachers could also have the class brainstorm a list of possibilities; e.g. a performing dolphin, a police dog, teaching a parrot to talk, training a racehorse.

• Model the planning and writing of an explanation using the framework on page 61. The pupils can then follow this example to plan and write their explanations about training an animal.

• Pupils could present their explanations about animals on colourful posters to be displayed in the school library. (Display/Publishing)

• Pupils could present their explanations as talks to the class, highlighting some of the specific terms used in training animals; e.g. 'drop', 'sit' etc. (Audience/Purpose)

Answers

Page 60

1. Teacher check
2. Teacher check
3. (a) Answers may include: think, act, begins, teach, help, visiting, handle, learn, move, meets etc.
   (b) Answers may include:
      • guide dog associations, breeds, stable temperaments, puppy raisers, public transport, busy places
      • one year old, tested, nature, intelligence, skills, training
      • harness, handle, commands, forward, instructor, disobey, learn to ignore
      • new owner, team, harness, normal dog
   (c) Teacher check
4. Teacher check

Extraordinary dogs

A guide dog is an animal that has been specially trained to act as the eyes of its visually impaired owner.

Guide dogs are usually bred by guide dog associations and are most likely to be Labrador retrievers, golden retrievers or German shepherds—breeds considered to have the most stable temperaments. A guide dog puppy begins its training at about eight weeks old, when it goes to live with people called 'puppy raisers'. Puppy raisers not only house train the puppy and teach it basic obedience, they also help it to get used to riding in public transport and visiting busy places like shops. These are things a guide dog must be able to handle with ease.

When a guide dog puppy is about a year old, it is tested to see if it has the nature, intelligence and skills to be a guide dog. If so, it begins demanding training that lasts about three to five months.

In the first part of the training, an instructor gets the dog used to wearing a harness and handle and teaches it commands like 'forward'. One of the most difficult skills the dog must learn is to disobey an instructor's command, if following the command will lead the instructor into danger. For example, if the dog has been told to go 'forward' onto a street, but there is a car coming, it should not move. A guide dog must also learn to ignore interesting smells, noises and other animals—things that dogs naturally find irresistible!

In the second part of the training, the dog meets its new owner and the two begin to work together as a team. The dog also learns that whenever its harness is on, it has to work, but when it comes off, it can behave just like a normal dog, having fun with its owner.

Guide dogs are a vital part of life for many visually impaired people. They help to provide independence and confidence in a unique way.

Use the explanation on page 59 to complete the page.

1. Title

Suggest an alternative title for this explanation.

2. Definition

Rewrite the definition in your own words.

3. Description

(a) Most of the verbs in an explanation are in the present tense: e.g. walk, jump. List three present tense verbs used in this text.

_____ _____ _____

(b) List three keywords or phrases from each paragraph in the description.

(c) Do you think the order of these paragraphs made sense? **yes no**

Explain your answer. _____

_____

_____

_____

4. Conclusion

Write a new conclusion for this text that contains an interesting comment.

_____

_____

1. Plan an explanation about how an animal is trained to do something.

Title

Definition

State the animal and what it is trained to do.

Description

How is the animal trained?

Conclusion

Ending with an interesting comment.

2. Write your explanation.

3. Edit your work.

Structural and language features are shown on the left and right of the text below.

Title	**Keeping cats indoors**	
Introduction – one or more sentences that state the problem and the writer's position	Dear community member I would like all cat owners in the local area to please consider keeping their pets indoors. There are many reasons why you **should** do this.	• a variety of controlling and emotive words; e.g. **should, murder**
Arguments – presented in logical manner with supporting details, usually from strongest to weakest	• Our native wildlife is at risk. Cats are skilful hunters designed to sneak up and expertly kill small prey like birds and small mammals. Just one cat could **murder** many animals in one day. Some of the animal species in our area are endangered and cats could make them extinct. We must stop this. Many people think that putting a bell on their cat's collar will stop them from stalking prey, but don't be fooled. Cats can learn to move in ways that stops their bells from making a sound. • Cats themselves are at risk. Your precious pets are in constant danger of being run over by cars, getting into fights with other cats and being hurt by larger animals or uncaring people who don't like cats. An injured cat may hide for days and never find its way back home. • Cats are happy inside. Unlike dogs, domestic cats are bred to be indoor pets. There is no reason why they should go outside **if** they are provided with interesting toys **and** given play time by their owners. Some people even go to the trouble of building 'cat runs' from chicken wire in their backyards. Responsible pet owners should be responsible for the happiness of their animals and cats are no exception to this.	• paragraphs used to state and elaborate on each point • a variety of conjunctions; e.g. **if, and**
Conclusion – restates the writer's position	It is time we as a community considered the dangers of letting cats roam outside. Please think twice before you let your cat outside again.	

Teacher information

- Discussions argue for a particular position and attempt to persuade an audience to share this view. This particular discussion is in the form of an advertising flyer.

- Members of the class could take turns to read this text aloud, or the pupils could read it independently.

- Identify the structural and language features indicated above before the pupils complete the analysis on page 64.

- Teachers should hold a class discussion about some appropriate community issues the pupils could write their discussions about. Pamphlets, leaflets or other advertising material produced by community groups, may provide further information or ideas for the pupils.

- Model the planning and writing of a discussion using the framework on page 65. The pupils can then follow this example to plan and write their discussions about community issues.

- Read local newspapers to find current community issues. Pupils could write a letter to the editor of the newspaper expressing their views. (Publishing/Purpose)

- Use discussion topics as the basis for debates on issues covered in geography lessons. Teachers could introduce debating speeches as spoken discussions. (Audience/Purpose/Context)

Answers

Page 64

1. Keeping cats indoors

2. Answers might include: community member, cat owners, local area, pets, indoors

3. (a) (i) Cats can kill native wildlife and could make some species extinct. Putting a bell on a cat's collar does not help.

   (ii) Cats who go outside are at risk of being hurt. Injured cats may not find their way home.

   (iii) Cats are happy inside as long as they have toys and play time with their owners. Cat owners should be responsible for the happiness of their pets.

   (b) Teacher check

4. Teacher check

Keeping cats indoors

Dear community member

I would like all cat owners in the local area to please consider keeping their pets indoors. There are many reasons why you should do this.

- Our native wildlife is at risk. Cats are skilful hunters designed to sneak up and expertly kill small prey like birds and small mammals. Just one cat could murder many animals in one day. Some of the animal species in our area are endangered and cats could make them extinct. We must stop this. Many people think that putting a bell on their cat's collar will stop them from stalking prey, but don't be fooled. Cats can learn to move in ways that stops their bells from making a sound.

- Cats themselves are at risk. Your precious pets are in constant danger of being run over by cars, getting into fights with other cats and being hurt by larger animals or uncaring people who don't like cats. An injured cat may hide for days and never find its way back home.

- Cats are happy inside. Unlike dogs, domestic cats are bred to be indoor pets. There is no reason why they should go outside if they are provided with interesting toys and given play time by their owners. Some people even go to the trouble of building 'cat runs' from chicken wire in their backyards. Responsible pet owners should be responsible for the happiness of their animals and cats are no exception to this.

It is time we as a community considered the dangers of letting cats roam outside. Please think twice before you let your cat outside again.

Examining discussion 1

Use the discussion on page 63 to complete the page.

1. Title

Write the title.

2. Introduction

List four keywords or phrases from the introduction.

_____ _____

_____ _____

3. Arguments

(a) Write a summary of each argument in this section of the discussion.

(i)	(ii)	(iii)

(b) Write the number of the paragraph
you think contains the weakest argument. _____

Explain your choice.

_____

_____

_____

_____

4. Conclusion

Add a final sentence to the conclusion that you think states the writer's point
of view very strongly.

_____

_____

1. Plan a discussion about a change you would like to see in your community.

Title

Introduction

State the problem and your point of view.

Arguments

List each argument you will use, starting with the strongest one.

Conclusion

End by restating your point of view.

2. Write your discussion.

3. Edit your work.

Structural and language features are shown on the left and right of the text below.

Title	Barking mad
Introduction – one or more sentences that state the issue and the writer's position.	It would be fair to say that audiences were not expecting much from Petrina Daro's new musical *Dogs*, **which** opened at the Finlay Theatre this week. Her past efforts have always been boring disappointments. **But** the spectacle that exploded onto the stage last night was a mad, joyful treat that should be seen by the whole family.
Arguments – presented in logical manner with supporting details, usually from strongest to weakest	From the moment the curtain opened, the nimble actors took on the roles of dogs with amazing accuracy. After only a few minutes of watching their actions, it was difficult to believe you were watching humans in costumes. Every singing voice was perfectly on pitch and matched the type of dog being portrayed. A favourite with the audience was the deep voice of Grif, the Great Dane.
	The rubbish dump set had also been well designed, with the actors appearing at different heights throughout the musical—on top of rusted out cars, inside old tyres, rolling in puddles and even swinging from cranes. Bright, bold colours were used, which made it impossible to tear your eyes away from the stage.
	The orchestra, conducted by Jane Overington, was simply glorious. A huge range of music was played by the expert musicians, from slow and haunting ballads to up-beat rock numbers.
Conclusion – restates the writer's position	It would be a **crime** to miss this amazing family musical. Do whatever you can to grab some tickets before the season is sold out. This **must** be the most awe-inspiring musical that has been written in years.

- a variety of conjunctions; e.g. **which, But**

- paragraphs used to state and elaborate on each point

- a variety of controlling and emotive words; e.g. **crime, must**

Teacher information

- Discussions argue for a particular position and attempt to persuade an audience to share this view. This particular discussion is in the form of a critical review.

- Members of the class could take turns to read this text aloud, or the pupils could read it independently. A class discussion could then be held about some other aspects of a performance a critic could comment on.

- Identify the structural and language features indicated above before the pupils complete the analysis on page 68.

- Model the planning and writing of a discussion using the framework on page 69. The pupils can then follow this example to plan and write their discussions.

- Pupils could present their discussions as speeches to other classes. (Purpose/Audience)

- Have each pupil compare his/her discussion with a pupil who expressed the opposite point of view. (Purpose/Audience)

- The topic could be debated by teams selected on the basis of the strength and conviction of the arguments presented in their discussions. (Context)

Answers

Page 68

1. (a) Barking mad

   (b) Answers should indicate that the word 'barking' was chosen because the review is about the musical, *Dogs*.

2. (a) and (d) should be ticked.

3. Paragraph 1   How the actors moved and sang

   Paragraph 2   What the set looked like

   Paragraph 3   What the musical score and the orchestra were like

4. (a) crime, amazing, grab or awe-inspiring

   (b) (i) should

       (ii) Do

Barking mad

It would be fair to say that audiences were not expecting much from Petrina Daro's new musical *Dogs*, which opened at the Finlay Theatre this week. Her past efforts have always been boring disappointments. But the spectacle that exploded onto the stage last night was a mad, joyful treat that should be seen by the whole family.

From the moment the curtain opened, the nimble actors took on the roles of dogs with amazing accuracy. After only a few minutes of watching their actions, it was difficult to believe you were watching humans in costumes. Every singing voice was perfectly on pitch and matched the type of dog being portrayed. A favourite with the audience was the deep voice of Grif, the Great Dane.

The rubbish dump set had also been well designed, with the actors appearing at different heights throughout the musical—on top of rusted out cars, inside old tyres, rolling in puddles and even swinging from cranes. Bright, bold colours were used, which made it impossible to tear your eyes away from the stage.

The orchestra, conducted by Jane Overington, was simply glorious. A huge range of music was played by the expert musicians, from slow and haunting ballads to up-beat rock numbers.

It would be a crime to miss this amazing family musical. Do whatever you can to grab some tickets before the season is sold out. This must be the most awe-inspiring musical that has been written in years.

Use the discussion on page 67 to complete the page.

1. Title

(a) Write the title. _____

(b) Why do you think the writer chose this title?

_____

_____

2. Introduction

Tick the information the introduction gives us.

(a) It tells us what is being reviewed. ☐

(b) It gives the writer's strongest argument. ☐

(c) It gives us the actors' point of view. ☐

(d) It tells us what the writer thought of *Dogs*. ☐

3. Arguments

Briefly explain what each paragraph in the argument is about.

Paragraph 1

Paragraph 2

Paragraph 3

4. Conclusion

(a) Discussions often use 'emotive' words— strong words that persuade the reader to do or feel something. Write two examples of these found in the conclusion.

(b) Discussions often use controlling words; e.g. 'You **must** go to the concert.' Circle the controlling word in each of these sentence fragments.

    (i) 'A mad, joyful treat that should be seen ...'

    (ii) 'Do whatever you can ...'

1. Plan a discussion that gives your point of view on the following topic:

'Which is better: listening to a music CD or a live musical performance?'

Title

Introduction

State the issue and your point of view.

Arguments

List your arguments, starting with the strongest.

Conclusion

End by restating your point of view.

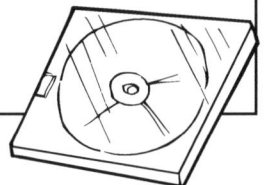

2. Write your discussion.

3. Edit your work.

Structural and language features are shown on the left and right of the text below.

Title		
	It's magic!	
Introduction – one or more sentences that state the issue and the writer's position	Dear Television Times Everyone seems to be talking about the new television show *It's magic*, in which the presenters reveal how famous magic tricks are done. Many people think the show is unfair to magicians and will destroy the mystery of magic, **but** I strongly disagree.	• a variety of conjunctions; e.g. **but, because**
Arguments – presented in logical manner with supporting details, usually from strongest to weakest	First, anyone who wants to find out how a magic trick is done just has to surf the Internet! There are hundreds of websites that explain how to do magic tricks. There are also many magic trick books. People can and do figure out how magic tricks are done eventually anyway—just by watching magicians carefully and concentrating. Shows like *It's magic* also encourage magicians to think up new illusions. This must be good for the magic industry. It means that people will continue to go to magic shows—to see more and more impressive tricks. The mystery of magic is not destroyed by *It's magic*. It is **ridiculous** to suggest that people go to magic shows **because** they think they are seeing real magic. They go to be entertained and ask themselves, 'How did the magician do that?'. It is similar to watching a film with special effects. Finally, *It's magic* **must** be encouraging younger people to get involved in magic, which seems to be a dying art. Magicians ***should*** be grateful that their art is being revived.	• paragraphs used to state and elaborate on each point • a variety of controlling and emotive words; e.g. **ridiculous, must, should**
Conclusion – restates the writer's position	Channel 12 should not take *It's magic* off the air. It makes fascinating viewing for all the family and also supports the magic industry. Yours sincerely Michael Lockhart	

Teacher information

- Discussions argue for a particular position and attempt to persuade an audience to share this view. This particular discussion is in the form of a letter.

- Members of the class could take turns to read this text aloud, or the pupils could read it independently.

- Identify the structural and language features indicated above, before the pupils complete the analysis on page 72.

- Model the planning and writing of a discussion using the framework on page 73. The pupils can then follow this example to plan and write their discussions.

- Pupils could create television magazines in small groups and include their discussions on a 'letters to the editor' page. (Publishing/Display/Context)

- Pupils could use their discussions as part of a script for a television interview presented to the class. (Audience/ Context)

Answers

Page 72

1. Teacher check

2. (a) *It's magic* is a show in which the presenters reveal how famous magic tricks are done.

   (b) The writer disagrees that the show is unfair to magicians and destroys the mystery of magic.

3. (a) People can find out how to do magic tricks by surfing the Internet, reading books or watching magicians carefully.

   (b) *It's magic* will make magicians think up more impressive illusions and people will go to magic shows to see them.

   (c) People go to magic shows to be entertained, not because they think the magic is real.

   (d) *It's magic* will encourage younger people to be involved in magic, for which magicians should be grateful.

4. Teacher check

It's magic! ☆

Dear Television Times

Everyone seems to be talking about the new television show *It's magic*, in which the presenters reveal how famous magic tricks are done. Many people think the show is unfair to magicians and will destroy the mystery of magic, but I strongly disagree.

First, anyone who wants to find out how a magic trick is done just has to surf the Internet! There are hundreds of websites that explain how to do magic tricks. There are also many magic trick books. People can and do figure out how magic tricks are done eventually anyway—just by watching magicians carefully and concentrating.

Shows like *It's magic* also encourage magicians to think up new illusions. This must be good for the magic industry. It means that people will continue to go to magic shows—to see more and more impressive tricks.

The mystery of magic is not destroyed by *It's magic*. It is ridiculous to suggest that people go to magic shows because they think they are seeing real magic. They go to be entertained and ask themselves, 'How did the magician do that?'. It is similar to watching a film with special effects.

Finally, *It's magic* must be encouraging younger people to get involved in magic, which seems to be a dying art. Magicians should be grateful that their art is being revived.

Channel 12 should not take *It's magic* off the air. It makes fascinating viewing for all the family and also supports the magic industry.

Yours sincerely

Michael Lockhart

Use the discussion on page 71 to complete the page.

1. Title

Write a new title for this discussion that tells us more about the writer's point of view.

2. Introduction

Write the two main pieces of information the introduction gives us.

(a) _____

_____

(b) _____

_____

3. Arguments

Briefly explain what each paragraph in the argument is about.

(a)

(b)

(c)

(d)

4. Conclusion

Write a new conclusion that restates the writer's point of view. Use some emotive words.

_____

_____

_____

Discussion plan ③

1. Imagine that your favourite television show was about to be taken off the air. Plan a discussion that argues why it should be continued.

Title

Introduction

State the problem and your point of view.

Arguments

List your arguments, starting with the strongest one.

Conclusion

End by restating your point of view.

2. Write your discussion.   3. Edit your work.

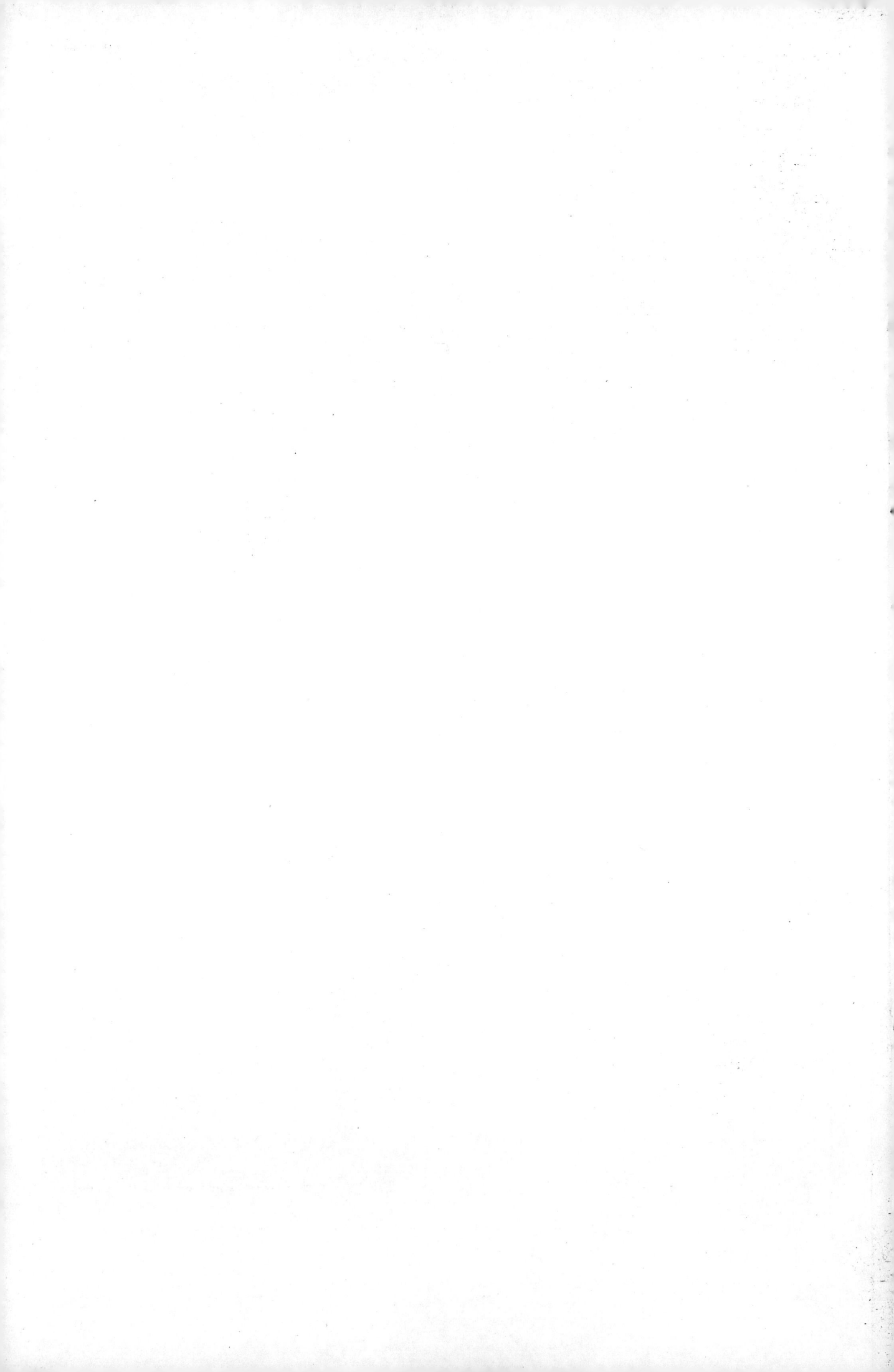